Our Title of Liberty

Our Title of Liberty

Latter-Day Politics for Latter-day Saints

Michael J. Snider

Easter Sunday, 2005

Al,

I consider myself fortunate to count you as a friend. Thank you for all you've taught me, both in word and by example.

I hope you find value in these pages.

— Michael J. Snider

iUniverse, Inc.
New York Lincoln Shanghai

www.ourtitleofliberty.com

Our Title of Liberty
Latter-Day Politics for Latter-day Saints

All Rights Reserved © 2004 by Michael J. Snider

No part of this book may be reproduced or transmitted in any form or by any means, graphic, electronic, or mechanical, including photocopying, recording, taping, or by any information storage retrieval system, without the written permission of the publisher.

iUniverse, Inc.

For information address:
iUniverse, Inc.
2021 Pine Lake Road, Suite 100
Lincoln, NE 68512
www.iuniverse.com

ISBN: 0-595-32533-5

Printed in the United States of America

Contents

Our Title of Liberty—Mission Statement vii
Chapter 1: The War (Referendum) in Heaven 1
Chapter 2: Politics Through the Ages 10
Chapter 3: "A Choice Land…Free from Bondage" 19
Chapter 4: "Politics from the Pulpit" 27
Chapter 5: From the Pulpit to the Ballot Box 38
Chapter 6: Befriending the Constitution = Conserving the Constitution 51
Chapter 7: Recognizing Attacks on the Constitution 61
Chapter 8: Separating the Wheat from the Chaff 73
Chapter 9: Discussing Politics, Religion (and other touchy subjects) 89
Chapter 10: Get Involved—Local, State, Federal…Pick One 98
Chapter 11: Cast an Informed Vote (In every election!) 105
Chapter 12: The 21st Century's Gadianton Robbers 114
Chapter 13: The "Just and Holy Principles" of the Constitution 122
Chapter 14: "When the Constitution is on the Brink of Ruin" 131
Chapter 15: Bringing the Constitution Back from the Brink 146

Chapter 16: "In memory of Our God, Our Religion, and
	Freedom, and Our Peace" 156
Appendix 165

Our Title of Liberty—*Mission Statement*

In the pre-existence, our first action of major spiritual consequence was also a political act...*we all participated in a campaign, and then cast a vote.* Ezra Taft Benson taught:

> "Some might even call the War in Heaven a political struggle—certainly it was controversial."—Teachings of Ezra Taft Benson, p.659

President Benson is teaching us something very important in this statement: that politics is not as separate and distant from religion as many would have us believe. He is reinforcing one of our basic beliefs; that as followers of Christ we believe in religious government, instituted by God, for governing worlds and universes (Abraham 3:2–3), and that we have an important role in sustaining that government. By the same token, politics is about governing too, and as Latter-day Saints it is part of our mission to ***apply*** celestial governing principles not just to church and self, but also to our earthly governments.

President David O. McKay, in his book *Gospel Ideals*, wrote that we all needed to work for the "establishment of divine government among human beings." How we carry out this charge will have an effect on how we are judged after this earthly experience is over. The 1st verse of the 134th section of the Doctrine and Covenants says: "We believe that governments were instituted of God for the benefit of man; and that *he holds men accountable for their acts in relation to them.*" Voting is an act related to government. We also know that we are commanded to seek out, uphold, and vote for "honest and wise men." *(D&C 98:10)*

Clearly Latter-day Saints have a responsibility related to political issues…but how can we be sure we're carrying it out? How can we apply celestial principles to today's confusing and complex political world? That's what this book is about, and here's how I came to write it…

We're taught that choosing the right is supremely important and that making righteous choices and taking strong spiritual stands is essential to our salvation. As I grew up I observed that the essence of politics and voting is the same as our spiritual tests—it's about making right choices and taking correct positions. But as I examined the issues and candidates I couldn't tell which were the correct choices. I felt like politics deserved more time and effort than I was giving it, or even *knew how* to give. Sure, some votes were fairly black and white when it came to big issues such as abortion, but there were a multitude of other candidate races and ballot issues where it was very hard for me to know what the proper choice of a good church member should be. We are counseled to ask ourselves: "What would Jesus do?" I believe it's perfectly reasonable to ask ourselves how a follower of the Savior would vote too!

This book will help you if you've ever felt the following self-doubts or questions:

- Whenever politics comes up in conversation, do you feel mostly unqualified to offer your opinion? (Mostly because you don't really have one of your own outside of repeating some slogan or phrase you heard from someone else or on television.)

- Have you ever felt like you needed others to tell you how to vote because you lack that special understanding of politics that will enable you to make the right choice on your own?

My initial answer of "yes" to those questions led me to do much searching and studying, and to spend a lot of time meditating and praying until I found the answers. I have spent my entire adult life studying politics and its role in the religious history of the world. I have run for my local school board twice, (unsuccessfully), and I belong to a number of community and political organizations. The principles I've studied, and which are set out in this book, confirmed and strengthened the testimony I already had of our Savior as the only way to return to God's presence. These principles also helped me to gain a greater awareness of politics and freedom, and an understanding that participation in government is an important part of our testing and trying here on earth. I discovered how political systems that hold the individual's freedom as their highest ideal, while respecting the liberties of others, provide the most ideal circumstances for men and women to become converted to the Gospel of Jesus Christ. I learned about the unique parallels between politics and the true doctrine of Christ that give Latter-day Saints a natural advantage in learning and practicing politics.

The purpose of this book then is threefold:

1. To help us as followers of Jesus Christ to dedicate ourselves to actively promoting the political conditions that will enable everyone, everywhere to gain access to His Gospel.

2. To heed the commandment given in the 98th and 134th sections of the Doctrine & Covenants to "Befriend...that law which is the constitutional law of the land."

3. To assist in fulfilling the prophecy of Joseph Smith that we may do our part to "bear the Constitution away from the very verge of destruction."

Chapter 1

The War (Referendum) in Heaven

- **The Conflict**
- **What was the principal issue over which the war in Heaven was fought?**
- **How could there have been a war in the pre-existence if no one had a physical body?**
- **How was the war in heaven fought and won by the righteous?**
- **How can we use the knowledge about our "first vote" to help us understand today's political issues, get involved, and make the right choices?**

The Conflict

What a dramatic moment it must have been—our first crucial moment of truth in scriptural history: The war in heaven. Once we understand the spiritual and political lessons of that war, the issues involved, and how it was fought and won, we can follow through on our first courageous vote. That vote was a conscious choice to sustain God's plan. We can exercise that same agency and conviction not only to overcome sin and error, but also to navigate the waters of latter-day politics.

There are many scriptures that describe the events surrounding the war in heaven. I've taken most of those verses and woven them together into a few short narrative paragraphs that lay out the basic personalities and events leading up to the conflict. (This gives us a panoramic overview easier than listing each phrase of scripture, its reference, then continuing back and forth between quote, chapter and verse, etc.) Reading the story from beginning to end also illustrates that this seminal event was not so much a campaign for a plan as it was a individual struggle to determine our own personal destinies. There was never a question as to whose plan would be used…it was always going to be God's plan, as championed by Jesus. The war in heaven meant victory or defeat on a personal level for each participant—it determined who would receive a physical body and come to earth for testing (i.e. keep their first estate), and who would not.

"And God said: These I will make my rulers; for he stood among those that were spirits, and he saw that they were good. And the Lord said: Whom shall I send? There stood one among them that was like unto God, and he said: "Father, thy will be done, and the glory be thine forever. We will go down and we will make an earth whereon these may dwell; and we will prove them herewith, to see if they will do all things whatsoever the Lord their God shall command them."

And another answered and said: "Here am I, send me. I will be thy son, and I will redeem all mankind, that one soul shall not be lost, and surely I will do it; wherefore give me thine honor," which is my power, for he said in his heart: "I will ascend into heaven, I will be like the most High; I will exalt my throne above the stars of God." And the Lord said: "I will send the first." And the second was angry, and kept not his first estate; and also a third part of the hosts of heaven turned he away from me because of their agency.

And there was war in heaven; Michael and his angels fought against the dragon; and the dragon and his angels fought against Michael; and the dragon prevailed not against Michael for they overcame him by the blood of the Lamb, by the word of their testimony; for they loved not their own lives, but kept the testimony even unto death. Wherefore, because Satan rebelled against me, and sought to destroy the agency of man, which I, the Lord God, had given him, by the power of mine Only Begotten, I caused that he should be cast down. Thus Satan was cast out into the earth; and his angels were cast out with him. He became the devil, the father of all lies, to deceive and to

blind men, and to lead them captive at his will, even as many as would not hearken unto my voice. And he was called Perdition, for the heavens wept over him—he was Lucifer, a son of the morning!"
(In the appendix I have recreated these paragraphs with the book, chapter and verse for each phrase, to give the reader the comfort that I have remained true to the context in which they were written)
Let's examine how these important events set in motion the great struggle between good and evil in the second estate.

What was the principal issue over which the war in Heaven was fought?

The war in heaven was fought over agency and power

Two plans for returning us to the Father's presence were championed by two of God's foremost sons, Jesus and Lucifer. The two plans shared the same goal, but their methods were very different. Jesus' plan, (which of course was the Father's plan), allowed for us to come here to earth and be free to choose whether or not we would be obedient to God's commandments: *"we will…see if they will do all things…the Lord their God shall command them"* (Abraham 3:25). Then, after the mortal probationary period was over and the earthly portion of His plan was fulfilled, the glory would remain with God: *"Father,…the glory be thine forever."*

The central feature of Lucifer's plan was that we would not have the freedom to choose: *"I will redeem all mankind, that one soul shall not be lost, and surely I will do it."* Satan's plan also stipulated that he would get the honor and glory himself for accomplishing it. But there was more to it than just taking unearned credit; he was also seeking God's power. In the twenty-ninth section of the Doctrine and Covenants there is a key definition in verse 36 that reveals how Satan coveted power above all else:

"…the devil…rebelled against me, saying, Wherefore give me thine honor, **which is my power…"**

This scripture shows us that God's power lies in the fact that he is honored and all his creations except man!". We also learn that the honor was secondary—what Lucifer really coveted more than anything else was the power he thought would come with that honor. The great tragedy of the son of the morning was that he failed to comprehend his Father trying to teach him a supremely important principle: God's way of governing is *willing* obedience, not *forced* obedience! Satan refused to learn that God's creations obey Him because they honor Him, not because they're forced to. That's why the plan of salvation had to be based on free agency for the spirits sent to live here.

Satan would have none of it though. His megalomaniacal thinking is further revealed in the following passage written by the prophet Isaiah: *"for he said in his heart: I will exalt my throne above the stars of God."* This scripture reveals the full intent of Satan's plan—to get everyone to give up their freedom and honor Lucifer over the Father, so he could be exalted over all creation. What a pathetic desire on the part of a being to dominate his creator! At that point, God let us all know that His plan, as presented by his only begotten, would be the one to prevail; and that's when we cast that first vote as to whom we would follow...

Final vote tally:

The Father and Jesus' Plan of Happiness and Salvation:	66%
Satan's Plan of Forced Obedience:	33%

How could there be a war in the pre-existence if none of the participants had a physical body?

> *"And there was war in heaven; Michael and his angels fought against the dragon; and the dragon and his angels fought against Michael; and the dragon prevailed not against Michael..." (JST Revelation 12:6–7)*

when we hear the word "war," we tend first to think of some kind of physical warfare, akin to what we read about in history, with swords, guns, bombs, etc. We know that as pre-existent spirits, we did not possess bodies, so it's important to realize that the war in Heaven was not a physical war, (for how could we wield arms and weapons?), but a battle of ideas, principles, testimonies, words and personalities. For our purposes, think of the word "war" as it is used to describe other conflicts; i.e., a "war of words," or a "war of opinions," or an "ideological war," etc.

Sometimes I refer to the conflict in the preexistence as "the referendum in heaven" not in an attempt to trivialize it, but to highlight its political aspects. It also helps me to remember that **today's war between good and evil must be fought much the same way it was fought in the preexistence.** The apostle Paul described the conflict on earth as follows: "For we wrestle not against flesh and blood, but against principalities, against powers, against the rulers of the darkness of this world, against spiritual wickedness in high places." Another reason I think of that first preexistent choice as a vote is to help me remember that the choice was ours then, and still is today—to freely make our choice and then back it up with our actions.

Today, just like the preexistence, we are in a war between good and evil, and just like then, the war is not being fought with bombs, guns or swords. Satan still uses much the same battle plan for enslaving the souls of men as he did in the preexistence: the flaxen cords of subtle deceit, lies, and false promises. If we fail to understand the nature of the war in heaven and its similarities to the one we're fighting every day, then we've given up one of our most important advantages over the enemy.

How was the war in heaven fought and won by the righteous?

> *"For they have overcome him (Satan)…by the blood of the Lamb, by the word of their testimony; for they loved not their lives, but kept the testimony even unto death…"* Revelations 12:11

After the two plans were presented we probably took time to discuss the merits of each one. The pros and cons were most likely brought up as we got involved to one degree or another in that heavenly council. As that scene unfolded it probably became clearer and clearer who would follow the Father and Jesus, and who would rebel against the plan of happiness. Then came the war, fought by two distinct adversarial forces that banded together around two distinct and opposing ideas. Those obedient to the Father possessed the overwhelming love and atoning sacrifice of the Only Begotten of the Father as both their sword and shield. The other side had Satan's suffocating pride, swift intellect and insatiable drive to dominate the souls of men as their primary tool of warfare. Heavenly Father had already announced which plan was to be used, so what was really being fought was the battle for each individual soul. Imagine the scene as some spirits hesitated and others changed their allegiance. It was truly a battle of life and death!

The following are my own ideas about the kinds of exchanges that might have taken place between the two opposing sides:

- "Under the Father's plan, we will get physical bodies and the freedom to do with them as we wish!"
- "But if we follow Jesus' plan, we might not make the right choices; whereas under Satan's plan, we'll all get bodies, and we'll all get back to Heaven!"

- "Yes, Jesus' plan carries risk; but what will it be worth if we all make it back, having been forced in every important decision of our earthly lives?"

- "Can't you see that the decision's already been made anyway? God has already told a small group of us that he will make them his rulers. (Abraham 3:23) It's not fair for some to return to the Father's presence while others cannot…it's discrimination!"

- "How can you ignore the great sacrifice of the Lamb? Don't you believe what He and the Father have promised us?" "I would rather live free to take advantage of the great sacrifice Jesus will perform on our behalf than live as a slave to Satan for the rest of my existence!"

As the scripture says, Michael, together with his angels won the war in Heaven using two related weapons:

1. "The blood of The Lamb," or the atonement of Jesus Christ, and
2. Our testimonies of Christ's atonement, which we kept, "even until death."

The dictionary describes testimony as a "profession or declaration of religious faith." Those unfamiliar with the power of a testimony of truth might not understand how a testimony can win hearts and minds. Monthly fast and testimony meetings give Latter-day Saints a firm grasp of what saying the truth out loud can accomplish, especially when accompanied by the Spirit of Truth.

Imagine that you might have had a discussion with one of the proponents of Satan's plan that went something like this:

Lucifer's campaign worker: "How do you **know** that Jesus won't commit any sin and that he will work out the perfect atonement he promised?"
You: "I don't know for sure. I have faith that he will."
Lucifer's campaign worker: "How do you know that you'll be capable of the kind of repentance and obedience necessary to get back to the Father?"
You: "As I said, I don't know for sure, but I do have faith in Heavenly Father and Jesus' promise, that if I make my absolute best effort to live by God's word then His grace will provide what I lack so that I may return."
Lucifer's campaign worker: "What if they don't keep that promise?"
You: "I have seen the actions, and felt the spirit of both Jesus and of Lucifer and I can judge between the two. I already have a testimony of my Savior; I

know he will lead me along the path of righteousness. I know that if I follow Him, He will teach me on earth through the Holy Spirit just as He is teaching me here!"

That's just one possibility of how we overcame Satan and his minions by using our testimonies. What a campaign! (Interesting isn't it…the word "campaign" is used to describe both war battles and political contests) We heard two separate plans from two potential leaders, both claiming that their plan offered the opportunity to return to the Father's presence to enjoy eternal happiness. Then those who had opted to choose the right, using only their testimony of God's true plan, coupled with a willingness to die defending that plan, won the day. In the end, it was our vote of faith in Jesus and his championing of God's plan that gave us the victory, and won us our free agency. The casualties were those souls who will never know any degree of glory because they chose Satan's plan.

We overcame Lucifer and his forces by drawing on our testimony of the atonement of Jesus Christ. The scripture says, we kept that testimony "even until death," so some kind of death must have been possible and we must have been able to fear it. I believe that the death we feared was the spiritual death that would result from not being valiant enough to keep our first estate…a death that would forever separate us from our Father's glory. Even though we feared that death, we summoned the courage to stand up to those who wanted to take our freedom from us. The faithful caught hold of the vision of Christ's magnificent and eternal sacrifice and fought for the freedom to live for Him—because we knew He would die for us—and stood firm in the face of those who would try to take away that opportunity.

The Lord described the preexistent victory scene to Job: "…the morning stars sang together, and all the sons of God shouted for joy…" (Job 38:7) I imagine we were so happy because we had just won a triumphant victory over evil. I like to think that a big part of that happiness came from the knowledge we now possessed that we could do it! It's one thing to have faith and feel confident in doing something, and it's another to actually go out and accomplish it. In the war in heaven we risked our spiritual lives to defend the God's plan and as a result, experienced the first big fulfillment of our faith. We also knew that this was only the first time we would be called to fight this battle. Winning our first estate did not assure us a place in the Celestial Kingdom, it gained us the opportunity to come to earth and fight the same battle in the flesh. That high reward now awaits those who successfully repeat that victory in this, the second estate.

How can we use the knowledge about our "first vote" to help us understand today's political issues, get involved, and make the right choices?

Two thirds of us chose to assume the risks that came with freedom to follow God's plan. One third of the preexistent spirit children gave up that agency for the supposed "security" of Satan's plan. If you're here on earth reading this book, then you were a combatant in that war in heaven...**and you were on the winning side!**

In the preexistence you believed enough in Jesus' atonement to use it as a weapon of personal strength to defend against the forces of evil. Even though you can't remember it exactly, that inner spiritual conviction of what is right and just will also serve you in this life as a means of fighting difficult battles as you try to sort out your political decisions and actions. Testimonies are used in politics too. The side that presents the true message plainly and passionately, coupled with the deeds to back up its testimony ultimately wins the war, (even though some smaller battles are lost along the way). But the side of right must always rely on heavenly principles: persuasion, longsuffering, gentleness and love. The minute we try to exercise force, Satan is pleased because we're using his methodology. The following quote by Elder Ezra Taft Benson eloquently expresses both the love and logic of this principle:

> *"We believe the gospel is the greatest thing in the world; why then do we not force people to join the Church if they are not smart enough to see it on their own? Because this is Satan's way not the Lord's plan. The Lord uses persuasion and love."*
> Ezra Taft Benson, Conference Report, April 1965, p.123

There are other spiritual implications and principles that can be learned from the war in heaven, but for us as latter-day political students, it's most important to understand that righteousness, freedom and personal agency are the winning combination in this conflict. We'll be returning to that combination again and again throughout this book, because even though the war in heaven is over, Satan continues to fight it:

> *"The war in heaven was a war of ideologies...and so it is in the warfare of the world today...It is a continuation of the war in heaven."*
> Bruce R. McConkie, The Millennial Messiah, p.696–p.697

Lucifer has not given up on the 66% of souls that rejected him; he's still working hard to tempt us to voluntarily share his eternal misery by succumbing to his silky lies and flaxen falsehoods. Since you and I wouldn't accept bondage in the preexistence, one of Lucifer's principal goals is to trick you into voting for it here on earth. And just as in the preexistence, you and I are needed to continue the earthly fight to champion the Father's plan of salvation, happiness and freedom.

Chapter 2

▼

Politics Through the Ages

- **Political Systems Prior to the Founding of The United States of America**
- **Patriarchal/Tribal Government**
  - The Rebels of Noah's Day
  - The Obedient Followers of Enoch
- **Law & Judges**
- **Kings & Kingdoms**
- **Democratic/Constitutional**

The world's political history deals mostly with the same issues we fought for in the preexistence—our freedom and whom we allow power over that freedom. It's important to understand the different frameworks in which political power is exercised if we're to make wise choices regarding the power we give to those we elect. Our vote is our power and it behooves us to be careful in using that power for righteous ends. It's also important to be familiar with the basics of political history so that we can identify good governing principles and then apply them to new circumstances.

Political Systems Prior To the Founding of The United States of America

If politics is the art or science of guiding or influencing government policy, it's useful to look briefly at the basics of political systems from the beginning of history and then form our own political opinions and positions based on historically sound and enduring principles. For our purposes, we can boil down the different political systems since the world began to the following four categories listed in this chapter's head: Patriarchal/Tribal, Law and Judges, Kings and Kingdoms, and Democratic/Constitutional. These four types of government developed in roughly that order, then coexisted in different countries and regions as history progressed, with one practiced in some parts of the world while another system prevailed in another. It's important not to dwell too much on minor distinctions between them though. What will benefit us most will be to examine historically how members of the true church have *"Render[ed] therefore unto Caesar the things which are Caesar's; and unto God the things that are God's," (Matthew 22:21)* no matter which system governed them.

System #1—Patriarchal/Tribal

For roughly the first 2,000 years (up to the time when Jacob/Israel and his sons became the twelve tribes of Israel), the world was very free, politically speaking, and living under the patriarchal order that God established when Adam left the Garden of Eden. Under patriarchal government, all men were to obey the two great commandments: to love God with all their heart, and to be their brother's keeper, (i.e., love others as themselves.) They were commanded to rear their families in love and righteousness, offering prayer and sacrifice to God in similitude of his only begotten Son, who would come in the meridian of time to redeem all mankind from their sins. Under this order, righteous patriarchs governed the family of man using those two great commandments as the basis of their rule; with each individual patriarch expected, (but not forced), to obey and govern their own families accordingly.

Thus early in the earth's history, politics and choosing political leaders was mostly an extended family/tribal affair with the largest family-tribes constituting what today we would call countries. The most righteous sons (not necessarily the firstborn) inherited the spiritual and political mantle of leadership and that's how people lived and worked—and they were free to achieve and do whatever they wished. Some make the mistake of thinking that the people in the earliest eras of the world history were not as free as we are today simply because they did not enjoy the modern democratic institutions and technological inventions that we have today. Certainly life was much more difficult with regards to obtaining food, clothing and shelter, but that doesn't mean that they weren't free to live their lives as they wished. The patriarchal form of government was one of the most ideal periods in earth's history for the preaching of the Gospel because government was obviously minimal and mostly stayed out of the day-today aspects of people's lives. It is noteworthy that the freest political systems always provide the best conditions for the preaching and practice of true religion, which in turn create the most prosperous societies.

As with any other time in history, there were those who exercised their free agency to obey and those who chose to rebel against the order. It's important to remember that political upheaval in those days didn't happen as it does in our day. Today, those who disagree with the prevailing political system must start a revolution and take over their own homeland or invade another country. In those days the world was new and there was plenty of room for the disgruntled and disobedient to simply leave the patriarchal order, fan out and do what they wished in some other place under their own tribal order. We find good examples of both sides of this perennial political equation in two ancient patriarchal/tribal societies: those who disobeyed and revolted against Noah, and those who obeyed and followed Enoch.

The Rebels of Noah's Day

The political and spiritual rebels of Noah's time were pretty full of themselves. When Noah and his sons attempted to preach the gospel to those who had chosen not to follow the patriarchs, they were rewarded by attempts on their lives. Those who ignored Noah answered his call to repentance much the same way the secularists of today do when confronted with the invitation to repent:

> "...after that they had heard him (Noah), they came up before him, saying: Behold, we are the sons of God; have we not taken unto ourselves the daughters of men? And are we not eating and drinking and marrying and giving in marriage? And our wives bear unto us children, and the same are mighty men, which are like unto men of old, men of great renown. And they hearkened not unto the words of Noah." (Moses 8:21)

These rebels "voted" to reject the righteous government of the patriarchs. Their false arguments are similar to the falsehoods of those today that disregard history and thus advocate America's demise. They rejected Noah's call to repentance by citing that they were sons of God too, (as if the mere act of being sons of God automatically excused them from having to listen to God's prophet.) Their next rationale for rejecting God's counsel was that they were getting married, and that their sons and daughters were growing up to be "mighty men...like unto men of old...of great renown." I'll never understand how this was supposed to be an answer to Noah's preaching! Noah was urging them to repent and obey God and they replied that they couldn't be doing anything wrong because they were getting married and raising children, and somehow that meant that they had no need of repentance. Simply put, they "hearkened not unto *Noah's* words;" (Moses 8:20)

Similar worldly voices are operating today, except they claim we are children of a disembodied and disinterested God, (who they then try to eliminate from all aspects of public life.) They also try to convince us that they're following in the footsteps of "men of renown" such as the founding fathers, but upon careful examination, their words and actions bear little resemblance to anything these wise men ever said or did.

The Obedient Followers of Enoch

There were societies that obeyed the wise government of the patriarchs and flourished. Enoch was among the greatest of the patriarchs and there were rich rewards, both spiritual and temporal for those who followed him. At first Enoch balked at his call to prophetic leadership because he thought he was too young, that others did not like him, and that he wasn't a good speaker. (It's interesting to note that these are roughly the same objections some of us raise when asked to get involved in political or religious activity!) But God knew Enoch's righteousness and potential and told him to do as he had commanded; to open his mouth and "it shall be filled" (Moses 6:32). Enoch obeyed and became a preacher so powerful that when his enemies confronted him:

> "*...he spake the word of the Lord, and the earth trembled, and the mountains fled even according to his command...and all nations feared greatly, so powerful was the word of Enoch*" *(Moses 7:13).*

At the end of that verse we read what power God gave to Enoch so that he could accomplish these marvelous works:

> "*...so great was the **power of the language** which God had given him*". *(Ibid. bold, authors)*

Great speakers and writers have led great spiritual and political movements by using powerful words of truth and testimony. That doesn't mean that the flashiest or greatest orators are the only ones who can lay claim to powerful language. Enoch himself said that he was not a great speaker; his language was powerful though because he preached the truth. All of us need to be eloquent; not as the world would defines it, but as the Lord defines bold communication of spiritual and political truth by the power of His Spirit.

Enoch's mouth was truly filled with powerful language because he was obedient to God's commandments. Equipped with that power, Enoch founded one of the greatest societies in earth's history. He established a city of such righteousness, where the citizens followed with such exactness the commands relayed to them by Enoch, that "the Lord came and dwelt with his people." Imagine a people so in tune with God's laws and love that the Master himself could come down and linger in that city! They were also invulnerable to attack by the unrighteous. As the scripture says: "The fear of the Lord was upon all nations..." In other words, nobody messed with the city of Enoch! Enoch's people shone as a beacon of righteousness in the midst of a wicked world; "...and they were blessed upon the mountains, and upon the high places, and did flourish." (Moses 7:17)

The city of Enoch is a good example of a society that made conscious spiritual and political choices to follow righteous governing principles and was subsequently taken up into heaven to continue enjoying the pure love, peace and prosperity they had created.

> "...and it came to pass that Zion was not, for God received it up into his own bosom; and from thence went forth the saying, ZION IS FLED" (Moses 8:69).

System #2—Law & Judges

New conditions developed during the time of the patriarchs that necessitated the introduction of a new system of government. The earth's continental land mass had been divided in the days of Peleg, (*Genesis 10:25*), and from the scriptural record it appears that, due to the earth's baptism and cleansing in the days of Noah, the land mass now known as the western hemisphere was without inhabitants. The Americas were unpopulated, separated by an ocean from known civilization. The prophet Lehi tells us as much after his arrival in the promised land:

> "*And behold, it is wisdom that this land should be kept as yet from the knowledge of other nations; for behold, many nations would overrun the land, that there would be no place for an inheritance.*" (2 Nephi 1: 8)

Since the majority of the people on the earth had demonstrated that they would not follow God and be "as one," the concept of a covenant people was introduced through one of the greatest of the patriarchs, Abraham. God promised to bless the children of the covenant—provided they obeyed His commandments. The spiritual and political structure would then be set up so the covenant people could know the law they were to obey in order to enjoy the blessings that come from being a covenant people. Moses the lawgiver was just the prophet God needed to grow that system. But first, the children of Abraham would be tested and tried.

Shortly after the lifetime of Abraham, Isaac & Jacob, the covenant people were in bondage some 400 years to the Egyptians. The enslaved and impoverished conditions in which the Hebrew people lived produced a people in need of a strong government. The Jews had been deprived of their basic human rights and privileges for many generations; all so that the Pharaohs could build monuments to themselves. As a result, the plain and precious truths of the Gospel had languished. Led by Moses the lawgiver they departed the land of their enslavement to go inherit the land their father Abraham had been promised and started over from scratch religiously, economically and politically.

During their prolonged period of slavery though the children of Israel had become like little children. Without slave masters, the newly free people had no concept of governing themselves, so as they wandered in the wilderness there were many disputes of the same type found in any society: money, property, personal trespass, etc. Moses had to arbitrate every little disagreement among them and almost collapsed from the demands of this work until his wise father-in-law Jethro intervened. Jethro counseled Moses to choose wise men that "fear God, men of truth…to be rulers of thousands, and rulers of hundreds, rulers of fifties, and rulers of tens; And let them judge the people…and…bear the burden with thee." (Exodus 18:21–22). Soon after that, the Lord gave Moses the Ten Commandments, and the Law of Moses, which laid the foundation for the system of law & judges.

Of the three main societal achievements, religion, economics, and politics it should be recognized that the Jews built one of the greatest societies ever known on this earth. During the height of their obedience kings David and Solomon governed a mostly righteous nation while also building a thriving economy and strong political government. We owe a debt of gratitude for that example which we can both follow and learn from.

Law and Judges is one of the most ideal systems for governing men on earth, as it is a form of republic where rulers have charge over numerical divisions of the people. The advantage law and judges has over other republics though is that the laws are written by God's prophets so that corruption of the lawmaking process is not the danger it is when left up to man. This particular system should have governed the children of Israel for the next 1,500 years until the coming of Christ, but it only lasted for about 400. It is an important fact that free political systems require a strong and moral people to maintain them. The majority of the Children of Israel did not fulfill their part of the covenant so they languished in idolatry and wickedness until Israel split itself into two kingdoms. That division ushered in the next system of government which is possibly the most popular (in terms of usage) that the world has ever seen.

System #3—Kings & Kingdoms

At this point in the world's history, families, tribes, and allegiance to God, (or a God) ceased for the most part to be the focal point of government and men simply started using violence and the sword to set up one-man governments, i.e., kings, to decide exactly what the laws of the land should be. Some might argue that the Pharaohs had been doing this for some time, but the Pharaohs had at least tried to claim priesthood authority to govern through Ham's patriarchal lineage. Kings and Kingdoms is not an automatically bad political system, (there have been many kings who reigned in righteousness), it's just that there is so much that can go so wrong so fast. (See the 29th chapter of Mosiah in *the Book of Mormon*.)

There's really nothing more to this particular system of government as it is the simplest and crudest of all—whatever the king says, goes, and the people can only hope that the king is a wise and good king. I consider all forms of socialism, fascism and communism as part of this category of kings and kingdoms. Nobody votes for a king and nobody votes to become a communist or socialist either. Socialists of all variants talk a lot about the "working class," and the "will of the people" but have never succeeded in the long term. Communistic systems are an endless series of 5 year programs which never deliver on their promises, but for which all the governed must sacrifice. Socialist/communist leaders are usually power-hungry individuals who hold life-or-death decisions over the people they rule with virtually no accountability. Communists might not hand off power to their own family members as kings do, but the government is still whatever the head socialist or communist says it is. All barbarian rule and dictatorships fall under this category heading also. That's why kings and kingdoms have been the most widely practiced form of government throughout earth's history—it is the default government for those who reject God and God's law as their ruler.

It should be noted that many modern monarchies are not the absolute power structures they once were. Most have some kind of parliament or congressional body that is elected by the people, with the king or queen as mostly a figurehead—Great Britain is a good example. England is a great democracy whose royal family has no real decision-making power over the lives of their "subjects." Great Britain, even though technically still a monarchy, is largely a democratic republic that should also be recognized for its great contribution to, and maintenance of, America's freedom.

System #4—Democratic/Constitutional

Democracy felt its first glint of sunlight under the Greeks and Romans, and briefly flourished in the centuries just prior to the birth of the Savior, but both collapsed due to a number of reasons, most of which can be traced to lack of a strong religious or constitutional foundation. Contrary to popular belief, pure democracy is not a great political system as it is technically nothing more than mob rule. In other words if you can get 51% of the people to outlaw free speech—then free speech would be eliminated and that of course is not a virtuous political system. Freedom and self-rule must be based on virtue, just as rule of oneself is not a ticket to do whatever one feels like doing. That lack of constitutional or religious foundation was the primary flaw that left the Greeks and Romans ripe for the taking by various barbarian kingdoms. Freedom to do anything is not a virtue; freedom to choose the right is what keeps men free. In the Doctrine and Covenants, the Lord explains his divine endorsement of the U.S. Constitution by mentioning the agency that accompanies it, but instead of putting the word "free" in front of it as we often do, he phrases it another way:

> *"That every man may act in doctrine and principle pertaining to futurity, according to the **moral agency** which I have given unto him, that every man may be accountable for his own sins in the day of judgment."* (D&C 101:78 bold, authors)

Fast-forward to 1776 when all the right circumstances came together to create the most enduring political and spiritual freedom the world has ever witnessed. The main contributing factors were the people who had come from Europe seeking religious freedom approximately 150 years earlier. Those early immigrants were familiar with the philosophy of John Locke and possessed a keen recognition of man's natural right to freedom of conscience and individual property rights, along with an innate belief in the potential goodness of man's nature as God's sons and daughters. Those early Americans played a crucial role in creating the mindset of American democracy that we enjoy today. Ultimately the wise founders of our nation came together, prayed, and then got to work hammering out two of the greatest declarations of government in man's history. In 1776 Jefferson, Franklin, Adams, and Madison and the founding fathers re-hoisted the Title of Liberty in the form of the *Declaration of Independence* and again in 1787 with the ratification of *the Constitution of the United States of America*. Our scriptural charge today is to honor the legacy of those wise men and to "befriend that law which is the constitutional law of the land." (D&C 98:6)

Chapter 3

"A Choice Land...Free from Bondage"

- The Scriptures boldly declare America's religious and political destiny
- Fate of Unrighteous Inhabitants of the Americas
- America to be Governed by Righteous and Free People
- The Prophet Mosiah...One of the First Authors of American Democracy
- The Pilgrims Come to Renew the American Covenant
- The Thanksgiving Tradition
- The First Thanksgiving—What Really Happened
- The Pilgrim's Experience Proved the Advantages of Freedom and Democracy
- America's Destiny

The Scriptures boldly declare America's religious and political destiny

In various Book of Mormon scriptures, the Lord declared America's destiny as a land of freedom from tyranny.

> *Behold, this is a choice land, and whatsoever nation shall possess it shall be free from bondage, and from captivity, and from all other nations under heaven, if they will but serve the God of the land, who is Jesus Christ…(Ether 2:12)*

That promise is both religious and political—the spiritual aspect should carry the most weight for all of us personally, but the political aspect cannot be ignored either; after all, being free from captivity or bondage by other nations is plenty political. The "American Covenant," as I call it, is that the Lord will maintain America as a land of liberty, free from bondage and captivity if its inhabitants will be righteous and serve him.

The earliest recorded instance that we have of the American Covenant is the one made with America's first post-flood inhabitants, the Jaredites. The Lord explained the covenant to the Brother of Jared when he told him about the promised land to which he and the others with him were to be guided:

> *And now, we can behold the decrees of God concerning this land, that it is a land of promise; and whatsoever nation shall possess it shall serve God, or they shall be swept off when the fulness of his wrath shall come upon them. And the fulness of his wrath cometh upon them when they are ripened in iniquity. (Ether 2:13)*

> *For behold, this is a land which is choice above all other lands; wherefore he that doth possess it shall serve God or shall be swept off; for it is the everlasting decree of God. And it is not until the fulness of iniquity among the children of the land, that they are swept off. (Ether 2:9–10)*

The Lord also extended the warning to those who were **not** members of his church, well in advance of their presence in America. The *Gentiles* would have a chance to be converted to his Gospel and enjoy the benefits of the American Covenant, and if not, they too would suffer the consequences. It is even more remarkable when one remembers that at the time the Lord gave this revelation there was no such thing as "Gentiles," as we define it today, (one who is not of the house of Israel), because the Jaredites left for America long before Jacob/Israel was born!

> *And this cometh unto you, O ye Gentiles, that ye may know the decrees of God—that ye may repent, and not continue in your iniquities until the fulness come, that ye may not bring down the fulness of the wrath of God upon you as the inhabitants of the land have hitherto done. (Ether 2:11)*

Fate of Unrighteous Inhabitants of the Americas

Ether 2:11 emphasizes God's tolerance toward the inhabitants of this land, as well as how faithfully he keeps his promises. He will put up with a lot, but if wickedness persists, he will have to sweep the wicked off or bring them into captivity so the righteous may possess the Americas.

Let's look at the fulfillment of the prophecy in Ether 2:11 with the following peoples:

Pre-flood Americans (from the days of the patriarchs)

- "…as the inhabitants of the land have hitherto done." Surely this refers to pre-flood people who were swept off the land by the flood in the days of Noah. No matter that the world was one landmass at the time. The land that would eventually break off and become the American continent was still the home of Adam's post-Garden of Eden dwelling and still held the same promise to both the righteous and the wicked.

Jaredites

- The Jaredites occupied the Americas from approximately 2,000 B.C. to 600 B.C. and were destroyed off the land by their own wickedness. They killed one another in massive wars of blind rage until there were only two men left. One was the prophet Ether, and the other was Coriantumr, the last of the combatants.

The Book of Mormon peoples, the Nephites and Lamanites

- The Nephites through their own wickedness were all killed, save a few, by the Lamanites after they disregarded the conditions of the American Covenant and engaged in the grossest sins and iniquities.

- The Lamanites, did not repent and were either driven from their lands or brought into captivity by the various European nations who were led to America.

The Prophet Mosiah…One of the First Authors of American Democracy

92 years before the birth of Christ, a Nephite king and prophet named Mosiah was trying to ensure the freedom of his people by asking them which of his sons should succeed him as king, (which is amazing in and of itself as kingly succession is almost never left up to the people.) None of his sons wanted to be king, so, instead of forcing one of them, Mosiah pondered how he might *"make for the peace of this people." (Mosiah 29:10)* The product of Mosiah's thinking turned out to be the first of the two great democratic republics on the American continent.

Mosiah devised a new constitutional democracy for the Nephite people, one in which the executive and judicial branches would be combined. There was no need for a congressional branch as the Nephites observed the Mosaic law which had come from God, thus they had no need for mortal lawmakers. Under Mosiah's system free elections were held for the various levels of judgeships, which could be compared to the district, appellate, and supreme courts of today, with the chief judge also serving as the chief executive. Under Mosiah's system, suspected lawbreakers were brought before the corresponding judge. If enough thought the judgment was in error, there was an appeal system whereby the case could be brought before a higher judge. If a higher judge's verdict was suspect, then a group of lower court judges could impeach the higher court magistrate.

Some ask, "In Mosiah's day, how did business, trade, and all the other things that are attended to by government today get taken care of?" The simple answer is that a moral and religious people, left to govern themselves, have no need of an intrusive government to take care of many of the functions we currently allow our government to get involved with. If that seems incredible, one need only go back seventy years or so to find much the same situation for most of U.S. history. The federal government's level of involvement for the first 150 years of our history was very minimal—just as the Constitution specifies. Hardly any of the government functions we have today existed before the 1930's, yet the United States of America thrived and grew.

Mosiah's thinking was the same as John Adams' and Benjamin Franklin's…that a free government depends on a moral and religious people, because without that critical element, any system of government, no matter how perfect in its form, will eventually crumble.

> *"Now it is not common that the voice of the people desireth anything contrary to that which is right; but it is common for the lesser part of the people to desire that which is not right; therefore this shall ye observe and make it your law—to do your business by the voice of the people.*
> *And if the time comes that the voice of the people doth choose iniquity, then is the time that the judgments of God will come upon you; yea, then is the time he will visit you with great destruction even as he has hitherto visited this land."*
> (Mosiah 29:26–27)

That scripture demonstrates the wisdom of that great prophet-statesman. Mosiah established a divinely based constitutional democracy that lasted approximately 300 years, through the coming of the Savior to America, and which endured until the wickedness of the people sealed their personal and national downfall. Mosiah was a man who knew and was committed to the American Covenant and who deserves a place in the pantheon of great American leaders along with the founding fathers of the American Revolution.

The Pilgrims Come to Renew the American Covenant

In 1620 the pilgrims came to America in search of religious freedom. These pioneers yearned not for an indiscriminate freedom lacking purpose, but the freedom to worship God according to the dictates of their conscience. They longed to build a shining city on a hill where any and all would be welcome to do the same. They were mostly English men and women who had first tried to settle in the Netherlands but soon realized that they would have to go to an entirely new and different land to obtain their goal. The story of the Pilgrims is important because it illustrates how the spirit of those 17th century Christians renewed the American Covenant and influenced the rebirth of righteousness, freedom, and democracy in the Americas.

The Thanksgiving Tradition

The current perception of Thanksgiving Day celebrated by millions of Americans is unfortunately, more tradition than fact. The true history of Thanksgiving was obscured long ago; even many of our history books are mistaken on this important story. The traditional version is as follows: The Pilgrims landed in 1620 and founded the Colony of New Plymouth. The first winter was difficult, but they survived with the help of the Indians. In the fall of 1621, the grateful Pilgrims held the first thanksgiving celebration and invited the Indians to a feast, complete with turkey and pumpkins. There was in fact a gathering with the Indians in 1621, but it was not a thanksgiving celebration, it was a shooting party. There was no Thanksgiving Day proclamation, nor any mention of a thanksgiving in any historical record of 1621.

The First Thanksgiving—What Really Happened

Anyone who wishes to read the pilgrims' true history can find it in William Bradford's "History of Plymouth." Bradford recounts how the Pilgrims came to America under a communistic property agreement in which all the pilgrims would own the land in common and share the harvests equally. By 1623, it became clear this system was not working out. Governor Bradford describes why:

> *"This community…was found to breed much confusion and discontent and retard much employment that would have been to their benefit and comfort. For the young men that were most able and fit for labor and service did repine that they should spend their time and strength to work for other men's wives and children without any recompense. The strong…had no more in division of victuals and clothes than he that was weak and not able to do a quarter the other could; this was thought an injustice…and for men's wives to be commanded to do service for other men, as dressing their meat, washing their clothes, etc., they deemed it a kind of slavery, neither could many husbands well brook it."*

The Pilgrims, being honorable people, would have continued under the communal contract they had agreed to before they left, but they were faced with starvation if they continued. They had to decide on a better way to govern themselves, or die. Governor Bradford describes how the solution was democratically devised:

> *"At last after much debate of things, the governor (with the advice of the chiefest among them) gave way that they should set corn everyman for his own particular and in that regard trust to themselves…And so assigned to every family a parcel of land, according to the proportion of their number for that end".*

The land was still owned in common and could not be sold or inherited, but each family was allotted a portion, and each family could keep whatever they grew. Bradford explains: "That had very good success for it made all hands very industrious, so as much more corn was planted than otherwise would have been."

By the spring of 1863, it was clear that the new capitalist system was a great success. The coming harvests looked abundant but during the summer the rains stopped and the crops were threatened. In an effort to save their crops, the Pilgrims held a "Day of Humiliation" and prayer. Soon after, the rains came and the harvest was saved. We can surmise that the Pilgrims saw this as a sign that God had blessed their new economic system, because Governor Bradford proclaimed November 29, 1623, a Day of Thanksgiving.

Thus, the first Thanksgiving Day was celebrated, the proclamation of which is found in Bradford's historical record. Much later, this first Thanksgiving Day became confused with the 1621 shooting party with the Indians.

The Pilgrim's Experience Proved the Advantages of Freedom and Democracy

In his Plymouth Colony history, Governor Bradford gave an excellent summation on why communism does not work:

> *"The experience that has had in this common course and condition, tried sundry years, and that amongst Godly and sober men, may well evince the vanities of the conceit of Plato's and other ancients, applauded by some of later times;* **that the taking away of property, and bringing into common wealth, would make them happy and flourishing, as if they were wiser than God.**" (bold, author's)

Note how Bradford scorns Plato and others who have put forth socialism as a virtue. He recognizes the conditions in which God placed us here on earth and states them plainly. Obviously man is not created on earth in communal groups with communal ownership of possessions. Men and women are born into *families*, each member of which must work "by the sweat of [their] face" to "eat bread." Governor Bradford hits the nail squarely on the head in recognizing the principal folly of socialism: It discards God's wisdom by relying on *man's judgment* of how to be happy on earth, instead of following the plan put forth by *the creator* of the earth.

America's Destiny

When one considers the histories of these various American peoples, it is plain that they were kept and preserved free when they obeyed God's law, and destroyed or brought into captivity when they disregarded His will. The latest, most free incarnation of the American Covenant has been established in the rise of the United States of America. We are inheritors of a rich legacy left to us by the men and women who came to America and reestablished the American covenant. The Founding Fathers and Mothers who created our country understood that this land has been reserved for a divine order that transcends the secular. They framed the state as a form of moral order because they knew that the keystone of moral order is religion. They also knew that without God, democracy could not long endure. In George Washington's first inaugural address that first great American president said:

> *"No people can be bound to acknowledge and adore the Invisible Hand which conducts the affairs of men, more than the people of the United States. Every step by which they have advanced to the character of an independent nation seems to have been distinguished by some token of providential agency."*
> George Washington, (from 1st inaugural address, April 30, 1789)

George Washington was among the first of many to recognize why it was so important to the Lord that the American Revolution be successful. Orson F. Whitney also understood:

> *"Were I to say that the founders of this Nation builded better than they knew, few if any would question the statement. But if, in addition to that, I should voice my conviction that this great Government was established purposely to favor the coming forth of the Church of Christ in this dispensation—the Dispensation of the Fulness of Times—many would deem my declaration presumptuous and even preposterous. Great movements are generally so regarded in the beginning. All great builders build better than they know. Some realize in part, but others not at all, that they are instruments of Deity, used for carving out his sublime and beneficent purposes."*
> Orson F. Whitney, Conference Report, October 1926, p.95

I hereby add my voice to those who proclaim America's spiritual and political destiny. This land, redeemed by the shedding of blood, has been set apart and preserved for a great purpose, and we as Latter-day Saints can strive to strengthen our conviction as we become more spiritually and politically active. Our responsibility is daunting only if we forget the battles that have already been won in the name of freedom and righteousness. If we are to "bear the Constitution away from the very verge of destruction" we would do well to study the great American patriots, both ancient and modern, and emulate their firm stand against those who would enslave America. Our vision, conviction, and defense of America as a free and choice land will make us part of the legacy of Mosiah, Washington, and Jefferson.

Chapter 4

"Politics from the Pulpit"

- **Early Church Political Involvement**
- **Joseph Smith's Candidacy for President & The Council of Fifty**
- **Prophets speak out on:**
  - **Communism/Socialism**
  - **Government Welfare Programs**
  - **Alcohol & Liquor Laws**
  - **Gambling**
- **We Must Follow Church Policy**

As I have grown up and dealt with the members of our church I have encountered a widely held opinion by many that the church doesn't "get political." This unfortunate assumption has justified many in separating their religion from their politics. It is also untrue because it implies that the church has no opinion on political issues outside of things like homosexuality and abortion. This opinion is also flawed because it supposes that government is involved in only a few moral issues, when in fact, it is involved in a great many. The official policy of the church is that it ***does not endorse political parties or candidates***, but it does indeed make statements regarding political matters. Prophets of God throughout the ages have called upon the members of the church to be active in peacefully challenging and shaping their governments so that they stick to "the things which are Caesar's;" so that men can render "...unto God the things that are God's." (Matt. 22: 21)

As best I can tell, the "church doesn't get political" assumption is a phenomenon of only the last 30 years or so. The church has been plenty political throughout most of this dispensation. Ezra Taft Benson said:

> *"The prophet may be involved in civic matters. When a people are righteous they want the best to lead them in government. Alma was the head of the Church and of the government in the Book of Mormon, Joseph Smith was mayor of Nauvoo, and Brigham Young was territorial governor of Utah. Isaiah was deeply involved in giving counsel on political matters and of his words the Lord Himself said, "Great are the words of Isaiah" (3 Nephi 23:1). Those who would remove prophets from politics would take God out of government."*
> Teachings of Ezra Taft Benson, p.138

Early Church Political Involvement

There were lots of politics mixed with religion during our church's early history; unfortunately most of it was very unpleasant. The state governments of Missouri and Illinois, as well as the federal government, failed to protect our prophet from murder by a mob. Religious persecution infringed on early church members' right to the free exercise of their religion, (as hard as that logic is to understand!). Because of that failure, most of the church's membership had to leave the territorial United States in order to escape property destruction and murder. That terrible trial, caused by government's failure in its primary function, made for plenty of political awareness among the Saints. We owe a debt of gratitude to those men and women who stood up for their freedoms, but who ultimately had to vote with their feet...literally.

When the pioneers crossed the plains in 1847 they settled on land that belonged to Mexico. Then in 1848 the United States won the Mexican-American War, after which the Treaty of Guadalupe-Hidalgo was signed, making the land settled by the Saints part of the United States of America. After Utah's application to become a territory was granted by the U.S. Congress in 1850, Brigham Young, the president of the church, also served as Utah's first territorial governor. Many political and church institutions were one and the same and were freely discussed in the press as well as from the pulpit.

In the church's post-pioneer era, the political focus shifted to the church's controversial position on matrimony. The church's insistence on a small percentage of its members practicing plural marriage pushed the issue to the forefront of the political dialogue of the day. Polygamy dogged the debate during the lengthy transition from territorial to state government as Utah petitioned for admission to the United States of America. Presidents John Taylor and Wilford Woodruff fought vigorously on political and spiritual levels until, just as had happened in Moses' time, *(see Matthew 19:3–8)*, God's law was altered because of man's hard-heartedness. President Woodruff issued *The Manifesto*, which signaled the church's compliance with the laws of the land regarding marriage.

The early 1900's produced church positions on evolution vs. creationism, the prohibition of alcohol, and socialism. Then two world wars saw the church throw its allegiance and resources into defeating Nazism and fascism. During the 1940's, 50's and 60's the general authorities preached against communism from the general conference pulpit. All in all, the leaders and members of the Church of Jesus Christ of Latter-day Saints have a rich history of being involved in, and speaking out on, the political front.

Church leaders and members have spent much time at the forefront of politics simply because that is where a good portion of the conflict of justice resides. Many aspects of politics and religion are simply inseparable. President J. Reuben Clark said:

> *"...today government has touched our lives so intimately in all their relationships and all these governmental touchings have been so tabbed as political, that we cannot discuss anything relating to our material welfare and existence without laying ourselves liable to the charge that we are talking politics."*
> Deseret News, "Church Section," June 16, 1945, p. 4., quoted by Elder Ezra Taft Benson, Conference Report, April 1963, p.111)

President Clark said that in 1945...Look at how many more "governmental touchings" we have today!

It is permissible, and even encouraged that church members unite to work on political causes. John Taylor, while he was president of the church, said:

> *"Let us stick to our covenants, and get as near to correct principles as we can, and God will help us. We want to be united in other things as well—**in our elections, for instance, we should act as a unit**. Other men are not ashamed to use their influence and operate in behalf of their party; why should we? As Amer-*

ican citizens, have we not the same right? Yes, we have. **Then let us be one and operate as one, for God and his kingdom."**

John Taylor, September 22, 1878, Journal of Discourses, Vol.20, p.59–p.60 (bold, author's)

Joseph Smith described his intentions to get involved and wield influence in political affairs on a February day in 1843 when the prophet went to the site of the Nauvoo Temple and addressed about 300 workers. In that talk, he made the following point:

"There is one thing more I wish to speak about, and that is political economy. It is our duty to concentrate all our influence to make popular that which is sound and good, and unpopular that which is unsound. 'Tis right, politically, for a man who has influence to use it, as well as for a man who has no influence to use his. ***From henceforth I will maintain all the influence I can get****. In relation to politics, I will speak as a man; but in relation to religion I will speak in authority. If a man lifts a dagger to kill me, I will lift my tongue."*
"History of the Church, Vol.5, Ch.15, p.286 (bold, author's)

And that's exactly what Joseph Smith went out and did.

Joseph Smith's Candidacy for President & The Council of Fifty

By spring of the following year, Joseph had declared his candidacy for president of the United States, drafted a formal political platform, and called upon members to serve in the campaign. In March of 1844 the prophet created the influential "Council of Fifty" to assist in his campaign and to function in other political matters.

"The Council of Fifty, a council formed in Nauvoo in 1844, provided a pattern of political government under priesthood and revelation…Members of the council understood its principles to be consistent with the ethics of scripture and with the protections and responsibilities of the Constitution of the United States. Non-Latter-day Saints could be members (three were among the founding members), but all were to follow God's law and seek to know his will. The president of the church sat as council president, with others seated according to age, beginning with the oldest…
The council, therefore, did not challenge existing systems of law and government (even in Nauvoo), but functioned more as a private organization learning to

operate in a pluralistic society. Its exercise of actual political power was modest, but provided a symbol of the future theocratic kingdom of God. Always, the Fifty functioned under the First Presidency and the Quorum of the Twelve Apostles, who were also members of the council."
Encyclopedia of Mormonism, Vol.1, COUNCIL OF FIFTY

In modern times, church leaders have spoken on many political topics, from the evils of communism, to drugs and alcohol, to social security/welfare spending. A good portion of this guidance has come from the pulpit at General Conference. Some has come through First Presidency declarations, as well as official statements in church publications. The wonderful thing about these statements is that they are plain to the understanding and free from the ambiguity that surrounds much political-speak these days. We can learn correct principles in forming our personal political opinions from the inspired words of prophets and apostles. We are then expected to go out into our communities and become actively involved.

The following statements by prophets, seers, and revelators serve to give us a basic understanding of the church's position on a number of important issues.

Communism/Socialism

President David O. McKay

> *"Communism is anti-Christ."*
> David O. McKay, Conference Report, April 1950, p.175

Elder Joseph F. Merrill of the Quorum of the Twelve

> *"We call upon all Church members completely to eschew communism. The safety of our divinely inspired Constitutional government and the welfare of our Church imperatively demand that* **communism shall have no place in America.***"*
> Conference Report, October 1946, p.72 (quoting from the 1936 1st Presidency "Official Declaration on Communism", bold, author's)

President David O. McKay

> *"On the flyleaf of the book, The Naked Communist, by W. Cleon Skousen, we find this quotation, and I admonish everybody to read that excellent book of Chief Skousen's: "The conflict between communism and freedom is the problem of our time. It overshadows all other problems. This conflict mirrors our age, its*

> toils, its tensions, its troubles, and its tasks. On the outcome of this conflict depends the future of mankind."...
> In their false teachings the Communists accept the doctrine of Marx who denies the existence of God, and repudiates man's immortality. Second, they deny the divinity of Jesus Christ and of course, his resurrection. They challenge the free agency of man."
> Conference Report, October 1959, p.5

Elder Ezra Taft Benson

> "The fight against godless communism is a very real part of every man's duty who holds the priesthood. It is the fight against slavery, immorality, atheism, terrorism, cruelty, barbarism, deceit, and the destruction of human life through a kind of tyranny unsurpassed by anything in human history. Here is a struggle against the evil, satanical priestcraft of Lucifer. Truly it can be called, **"a continuation of the war in heaven."**
> Conference Report, October 1961, p.70–p.71 (bold, author's)

Note how the brethren spoke against both the political and spiritual evil of Satan's plan; that's because the two are intertwined. The prophets of this church were among the first to denounce the evils of communism in large forums and publications. The members who followed that counsel played a large part in bringing about the demise of most of the world's communist governments. That's why I had to use quotes from 40–50 years ago—because Soviet communism has been discredited and eradicated due in large part to men and women who summoned the moral courage to speak against it and work to elect leaders who did the same. Don't assume though that because the Soviet Union is extinct that the fight against this particular evil is finished. There are a few communist countries still in existence that rule more than a billion of the earth's inhabitants and their evils are just as bad as they were when the prophets warned us about them.

Government Welfare Programs

The brethren do not condemn government welfare programs outright. They do make the distinction that the government variety is inferior to the Lord's welfare program though. It is clear that Latter-day Saints should not be advocates of expanding government welfare programs.

Elder Delbert L. Stapley

> "Welfare workers should make those helped feel good in receiving welfare assistance. Some claim humiliation in accepting help from the Church, yet are not embarrassed by receiving a government dole. The best antidote against humiliation is to furnish work opportunities for those receiving benefits in the program to give them the right feeling of having earned and therefore entitled to welfare assistance."
> Conference Report, October 1955, p.14

Elder Hartman Rector Jr.

> "Welfare lists grow daily, and we now face the startling fact that we have third and fourth generations growing up on welfare…Candidates for public office seem to be trying to out-promise each other in giveaway programs. As long as we in America have the mistaken idea that because we are born we have everything coming to us, Americans cannot solve this problem. Certainly the Lord speaks out strongly against able people who won't work but still expect to be fed."
> Conference Report, October 1975

Here's an insightful statement from the pulpit on what makes government welfare inferior to the Lord's program. Elder Benson zeroes right in on the spiritual aspect that flows to the correct political opinion:

Elder Ezra Taft Benson

> "Satan argued that men given their freedom would not choose correctly therefore he would compel them to do right and save us all. Today Satan argues that men given their freedom do not choose wisely; therefore a so-called brilliant, benevolent few must establish the welfare government and force us into a greater socialistic society. We are assured of being led into the promised land as long as we let them put a golden ring in our nose. In the end we lose our freedom and the promised land also. **No matter what you call it—communism, socialism, or the welfare state—our freedom is sacrificed.** We believe the gospel is the greatest thing in the world; why then do we not force people to join the Church if they are not smart enough to see it on their own? Because this is Satan's way not the Lord's plan. The Lord uses persuasion and love."
> Conference Report, April 1965, p.123 (bold, author's)

Elder Marion G Romney

"The practice of coveting and receiving unearned benefits has now become so fixed in our society that even men of great wealth, and possessing the means to produce more wealth, are expecting the government to guarantee them a profit. Elections often turn on what the candidates promise to do for voters from government funds. ***This practice, if universally accepted and implemented in any society, will make slaves of its citizens.****"*

"In Mine Own Way," Ensign, Nov. 1976, p.123 (bold, author's)

Elder Ezra Taft Benson

"No one has the authority to grant such powers as welfare programs, schemes for redistributing the wealth, and activities that coerce people into acting in accordance with a prescribed code of social planning.
…Once government steps over this clear line…into the aggressive role of redistributing the wealth through taxation and providing so-called "benefits" for some of its citizens, ***it becomes a means for legalized plunder.****"* (bold, author's)
Ezra Taft Benson, Conference Report, October 1968, p.19

Just after the Social Security program was initiated under FDR, Elder Levi Young gave a good explanation of why we as Latter-day Saints don't necessarily oppose the program, but should be wary of its potential for spiritual harm:

"The real test of the strength of civilization is in the moral capacity of the rank and file of the citizens to give up the pleasures of the present for greater rewards in the future. This quality is the foundation of both moral and spiritual character. The social security of a nation is based on the character of the citizens, not on the amount of material comforts the government may bestow upon them. Hard work and sacrifice make men strong. Ease and gifts from any source are destructive to efficiency, character, and citizenship. Social security is in the character of the citizens and hence must come from within. Social security cannot be bestowed from without."
Levi Edgar Young, Conference Report, October 1936, p.68

From the pulpit at General Conference, Elder Benson gave the following prescription for ***completely eliminating*** government welfare programs:

"Not all welfare-state programs currently in force can be dropped simultaneously without causing tremendous economic and social upheaval. The first step toward restoring the limited concept of government should be to freeze all welfare-state

programs at their present levels, making sure that no new ones are added. The next step would be to allow all present programs to run out their term with absolutely no renewal. The third step would involve the gradual phasing-out of those programs which are indefinite in their term. The bulk of the transition could be accomplished, I believe, within a ten-year period and virtually completed within 20 years."
Conference Report, October 1968, p.21

These statements show us that even though government welfare programs are not necessarily undesirable, they should exist only as temporary stopgap measures for the truly needy and not end up as they are today: large multi-generational, never-ending government programs that sap the moral strength of those they are supposed to help.

Alcohol & Liquor Laws

Prophets have preached in favor of government regulation of certain substances, one of the most damaging of which is alcohol. In fact, both the government and our church moved in the same direction as prohibition became an issue in American politics. The prohibition movement recognized alcohol as a moral evil that harmed families, while Latter-day Saints were being urged by church leadership to increase their adherence to the Word of Wisdom. Some are surprised to learn that before 1930, obedience to the Word of Wisdom was not a requirement for entering LDS temples or holding office in any Church organization. By 1930 though, abstinence from alcohol, tobacco, coffee, and tea became an official requirement for those seeking temple recommends.

Various general authorities spoke out on the evils of alcohol consumption and otherwise counseled church members to support the eighteenth amendment. Unfortunately an insufficient number of members heeded prophetic counsel and ultimately prohibition failed…with the people of Utah casting the deciding votes to repeal it. In the April 2003 General Conference President Gordon B. Hinckley poignantly recalled the effect it had on the president of the church at the time, Heber J. Grant:

"In 1933, there was a movement in the United States to overturn the law which prohibited commerce in alcoholic beverages. When it came to a vote, Utah was the deciding state.
I was on a mission, working in London, England, when I read the newspaper headlines that screamed, "Utah Kills Prohibition."
President Heber J. Grant, then President of this Church, had pleaded with our

people against voting to nullify Prohibition. It broke his heart when so many members of the Church in this state disregarded his counsel."
Gordon B. Hinckley, Ensign, Conference Report, May 2003, p.60

Gambling

Whenever gambling issues surface, such as referendums for state-established lotteries and casino licenses for certain ethnic groups, we Latter-day Saints already know how to vote:
Elder Dallin H. Oaks

> *"A few months ago, the First Presidency of The Church of Jesus Christ of Latter-day Saints made this statement:*
>
> *"There can be no question about the moral ramifications of gambling. As it has in the past, The Church of Jesus Christ of Latter-day Saints stands opposed to gambling, including government-sponsored lotteries. Public lotteries are advocated as a means of relieving the burden of taxation. It has been clearly demonstrated, however, that all too often lotteries only add to the problems of the financially disadvantaged by taking money from them and giving nothing of value in return."*
>
> *The first public policy argument against gambling concerns productivity. Columnist George F. Will explained it this way:*
>
> *"Gambling is debased speculation, a lust for sudden wealth that is not connected with the process of making society more productive of goods and services. Government support of gambling gives a legitimizing imprimatur to the pursuit of wealth without work."*
>
> "Gambling—Morally Wrong and Politically Unwise," Ensign, June 1987, 69

We Must Follow Church Policy

We are currently directed by our church leadership not to utilize church buildings or church phone lists to promote any political candidates or causes or imply church endorsement of parties and candidates and I wish to state in the strongest possible way that ***I do not advocate that anyone violate that policy.***

What I am saying is that the church is not "non-political" and never has been. Its leaders have never shied away from their duty to speak out as government has exerted influence over issues that affect the rise of God's kingdom. That is their calling—to speak out about just and holy principles, and those principles encompass all elements of truth, including things political. We have always been urged to put time and effort into carefully considering the issues, voting, getting involved, and otherwise exercising righteous judgment in these important matters. I firmly believe that we as a church membership are duty-bound to study the counsel we receive from the pulpit, and then become active in bringing it to pass in our nation. Our prophets have led the way in both word and example.

Chapter 5

▼

From the Pulpit to the Ballot Box

"Teach the people correct principles, and they govern themselves."
—*Joseph Smith Jr.*

- **Correct Principles Will Translate to Correct Voting Decisions**
- **General vs. Specific Instructions from the Pulpit**
  - **Examples**
  - **Racial Issues**
  - **Education and Education Spending**
  - **Subject Matter Taught in School**
- **Some Voting Criteria to Keep in Mind**
- **The Family: A Proclamation to the World—Political Ramifications**
- **"Of One Heart and One Mind"**

Correct Principles Will Translate to Correct Voting Decisions

This chapter deals with taking the counsel we hear from our leaders and implementing it.

Some people ask how Gospel principles can help us as we make up our minds regarding whom to vote for since the church does not support political candidates or parties. The answer lies in the quote I used as this chapter's subtitle: *"Teach the people correct principles, and they govern themselves."* We are to learn the just and holy principles resident in the Gospel of Jesus Christ and then use them to make our voting decisions. The prophet John Taylor, (who was also Joseph Smith's presidential campaign manager), gives us the context for that famous quote, and then expounds on its application:

> *What is it that will enable one man to govern his fellows aright? It is just as Joseph Smith said to a certain man who asked him, "How do you govern such a vast people as this?" "Oh," says Joseph, "it is very easy." "Why," says the man, "but we find it very difficult." "But," said Joseph, "it is very easy,* **for I teach the people correct principles and they govern themselves;***" and if correct principles will do this in one family they will in ten, in a hundred and in ten hundred thousand. How easy it is to govern the people in this way! It is just like the streams from City Creek; they spread through the valleys and through every lot and piece of lot. So it is with the government of God; the streams of life flow from the Great Fountain through the various channels which the Almighty has opened up, and they spread throughout the world, wherever there are any Saints that have yielded obedience to the commandments of God. The fountain is inexhaustible, and the rivers of life flow from the fountain unto the people."*
> Journal of Discourses, Vol.10, p.57–p.58, John Taylor, May 18, 1862 (bold, author's)

The prophet Joseph in effect said that good government will come from an ever-growing LDS population learning and practicing correct principles. As Latter-day Saints we are in possession of the "just and holy" principles of the Gospel of Jesus Christ and the U.S. Constitution (D&C 101:77), and we are spreading throughout the land. If we study the scriptures and our nation's founding documents we'll have all the knowledge we need in order to prepare for our ballot box decisions. (See chapter 13 The "Just and Holy Principles" of the Constitution.) It is also important to remember that what is preached from the pulpit at General Conference is scripture and this modern-day scripture will contain specific and topical principles for us to apply to our politics. Our responsibility is to apply the correct principle to the right situation in order to make the correct choice.

General vs. Specific Instructions from the Pulpit

It's important to know that the church will never tell us specifically how to vote because that would not be teaching correct principles and then letting us govern ourselves by our own agency. (There is the rare exception such as prohibition.) The prophet or apostles do not come out and explicitly say: "Latter-day Saints, vote for Candidate X or Proposition Z." The most specific they will ever get is to speak on certain issues and then leave us to our own free agency. President Gordon B. Hinckley summed up what the church does:

> *"...the Church will not dictate to any man how he should think or what he should do. The Church will point out the way and invite every member to live the gospel and enjoy the blessings that come of such living. The Church will not dictate to any man, but **it will counsel, it will persuade, it will urge...**"*
>
> *When I was a university student, I said to my father on one occasion that I felt the General Authorities had overstepped their prerogatives when they advocated a certain thing. He was a very wise and good man. He said, "The President of the Church has instructed us, and I sustain him as prophet, seer, and revelator and intend to follow his counsel."*
>
> President Gordon B. Hinckley, "Loyalty," Ensign, May 2003, p.58

As we saw in the previous chapter, church leaders speak from the pulpit on spiritual principles that are also political issues. They might address a given issue either directly or indirectly, but more importantly, they will *always teach the principle behind it*. In the last chapter we discussed prohibition, a constitutional issue on which church authorities spoke very specifically. Notwithstanding how passionately the brethren urged the members not to vote for repeal, they always expounded on the spiritual principle behind the church's position. Shortly after the twenty-first amendment (repealing prohibition) was presented to the states for consideration in February of 1933, Elder David O. McKay said in April General Conference:

> *"The world today perhaps as never before needs more spirituality. Booze and depravity mingle together harmoniously, but booze and spirituality, never. No one will contend that intoxicating liquors contribute spirituality either to the individual or to the nation. Nearly everyone concedes that intoxicants develop the baser, not the finer things of life."*
>
> David O. McKay, Conference Report, April 1933, p.92

All doctrine and commandments are taught this way. It doesn't matter if it's one of the Ten Commandments or a political issue. The brethren will not micro-manage our obedience. Elder Dallin Oaks taught in General Conference:

> *"Teachers who are commanded to teach "the principles of [the] gospel" and "the doctrine of the kingdom" (D&C 88:77) should generally forgo teaching specific rules or applications. For example, they would not teach any rules for determining what is a full tithing, and they would not provide a list of dos and don'ts for keeping the Sabbath day holy. Once a teacher has taught the doctrine and the associated principles from the scriptures and the living prophets, such specific applications or rules are generally the responsibility of individuals and families.*
> **Well-taught doctrines and principles have a more powerful influence on behavior than rules."**
> Elder Dallin H. Oaks, Ensign, Conference Report, October 1999 (bold, author's)

If we study the scriptures and the words of the Lord's anointed we will always be able to "judge righteous judgment" as we prepare to cast our votes.

Examples

The following two Gospel principles have been discussed in General Conference. Because the spiritual principles parallel political issues we can use them to illustrate how we can take "just and holy principles" and translate them into votes.

Racial Issues

The Book of Mormon teaches how, as a result of the Savior's ministry in the Americas, one of the principle elements of a Zion society is that there are no racial divisions:

> *"...**neither were there Lamanites, nor any manner of—ites**; but they were in one, the children of Christ, and heirs to the kingdom of God."* (bold, author's)
> *(4 Nephi 1: 17)*

There is no doubt that racism is one of the most divisive political issues facing America today. The liberal side of the debate says that in order to make up for the wrongs of the past, the victim's descendants must be compensated with quotas and racial set-asides, or rules that state certain percentages of jobs must be reserved for minorities. They also believe that "multi-culturalism" and "diversity" are virtues, and that a certain amount of segregation should be observed and perpetuated through special programs such as "black studies."

The conservative side believes that those living today, (who clearly had no part in creating the inequality), should not pay for past grievances. Conservatives also believe in the Civil Rights Act of 1964, and that we should all live, work and study together. Which side is in line with just and holy principles?

In his 1998 April Conference address, Elder Richard G. Scott gave a talk entitled "Removing Barriers to Happiness" and in that talk we find the formula for putting one's ethnic or cultural heritage in perspective. We also learn the correct political position on this very important and delicate issue.

Elder Scott began by explaining how he approaches this subject with the greatest of care and ends by apologizing if he has offended anyone. This is an important example of how certain issues need to be treated with great sensitivity when discussed with others:

> *"Increasingly the world is being divided into groups of individuals who seek earnestly to preserve their ethnic, cultural, or national heritages...Appreciation for ethnic, cultural, or national heritage can be very wholesome and beneficial, but it can also perpetuate patterns of life that should be set aside by a devoted Latter-day Saint...It is a violation of God's commandments for one culture to persecute another, whatever the reason."*

He then closes by illustrating the doctrine behind this important spiritual and political principle:

> *"Satan would segregate Father's children into groups with strongly held individual interests. He would encourage a tenacious preservation of those interests regardless of the consequences to others."*

From Elder Scott's profound explanation of the principle, we see how dividing the world into groups and pitting them against one another is Satan's primary tactic. We should identify those forces whose goal is not unity but division, and combine our influence against this practice. The Constitution is gender and color-blind. There is nothing in it that even suggests that different groups of people should receive different treatment or benefits based on their skin color or gender. Affirmative Action and other related quota systems create dependence and tear at the very foundations of the Constitution. Hence any kind of distinction or classification when it comes to college admission, job awards, etc., is unconstitutional, and not among those just and holy principles that we should seek to uphold.

In a 1917 General Conference talk, Anthony W. Ivins expressed how we should all unite under a common banner regardless of our national and ethnic differences:

> *"Just as this government is world-wide, and belongs to no race of people, so is the Church world-wide, and belongs to no sect or creed. Just as in the state the more exalted place within its gift is open to the humblest citizen, so in the Church is righteousness and good works the standard by which men are judged, and not by the heritage of birth. Like the State the Church says to all men, come unto me all you who labor and are heavy laden, and I will give you rest. But you must come as true Americans, leave behind the prejudices and traditions of the past, disavow allegiance to all other governments, you must support and defend the constitution of the United States..."*
> Anthony W. Ivins, Conference Report, April 1917, p.53

There is no question as to how we stand on the issue of race politics. All men are created equal, and if we are presented with a law or policy that attempts to treat various segments of people differently, we should vigorously oppose it. Orson F. Whitney said:

> **"All men are created equal."***...It does not mean, of course, that all men are equal in intelligence and capacity, any more than they are equal in stature or in weight. But all have equal rights to life, to liberty, to the pursuit of happiness, and are entitled to equal opportunities for possession and promotion.* **That is America's doctrine, and it is God's doctrine"**
> Orson F. Whitney, Conference Report, October 1926, p.94 (bold, author's)

To paraphrase Martin Luther King, Latter-day Saints know that all men will be judged not on the color of their skin, but on the content of their spiritual character.

Education and Education Spending

> *And as all have not faith, seek ye diligently and teach one another words of wisdom; yea, seek ye out of the best books words of wisdom; seek learning, even by study and also by faith.*—D&C 88: 118

Education is an issue that should be near and dear to Latter-day Saints in light of our belief that "the glory of God is intelligence." (*D&C 93:36*) Prophets and church leaders have consistently preached and championed the values of education.

In the last 50 years, education has become a major political issue regarding both its cost and its content. The reason it is a relatively new issue is because before World War II, education costs were mostly borne by those who directly benefited, i.e., parents and students. With the growth of the entitlement mentality though, the government's involvement in education and its funding has grown exponentially. Church leaders have given us valuable direction regarding sound principles that can help us prepare to vote in general, school board, and bond elections.

Cost

Money is the driving force behind many political issues and education is no exception. Here is a quote from President Hinckley in the October 1983 General Conference:

> "Now, while I am speaking of youth, I wish to say parenthetically just a word about education. I have great respect and appreciation for teachers. I am pleased to note that there is a public awakening to the need to prioritize our educational resources and programs...
>
> We have in the Church a strong tradition regarding quality education. Over the years we have allocated a substantial part of the Church budget to education, both secular and religious. As a people we have supported public education. Where there is a well-demonstrated need, we should be supportive. Such can become an investment in the lives of our children, our communities, and our nation. **However, let it not be supposed that all of the remedies may be found only with increased funding.** There is need for a searching analysis of priorities and a careful weighing of costs. Let us be supportive; let us also be prudent concerning the resources of the people.

President Gordon B. Hinckley, "Be Not Deceived," Ensign, Nov. 1983, 44 (bold, author's)

President Hinckley's comments are both prophetic and instructive as we witness the runaway costs of education. The U.S. spends more per child than almost all developed countries, yet lags far behind in test scores when compared to countries that spend much less per student. School board and bond elections certainly merit our close scrutiny in determining whether spending money is the right answer for every problem.

Subject Matter Taught in School

Public education curriculums used to be based firmly on reading, writing, arithmetic and history. Due to worldly influences, that foundation has become shakier and shakier. It's important that we let our local school district know that we support strong curriculums that are based on proven methods. A good example of this is the "phonics vs. the whole language" approach to reading. The phonics game didn't come out until the 1990's because there was no need for it. Before then phonics was the only method used for generations to teach children to read. Then in the 60's and 70's a methodology for teaching reading called "Whole Language" was introduced. This is a system that teaches reading by memorizing whole words, instead of learning to read and sound out words using their phonetic parts. Whole Language had been around for years and had never been proven to work, but because voters did not educate themselves, nor take the time to express dissatisfaction, the methodology was adopted. Whole Language then produced a generation of children, many of which could not read well; thus the free market saw the need and supplied the phonics game so parents could teach their children what most schools would not.

President Spencer W. Kimball explained that we should beware of these sorts of unproven concepts:

> *"BYU must resist false ideas. In this university (that may to some of our critics seem unfree) there will be real individual freedom. Freedom from worldly ideologies and concepts unshackles man far more than he knows. It is the truth that sets men free. BYU, in its second century, must become the last remaining bastion of resistance to the invading ideologies that seek control of curriculum as well as classroom. We do not resist such ideas because we fear them, but because they are false."*

The Teachings of Spencer W. Kimball, p.399

Sometimes I ask high school students what they know about important events in American history—the revolution, the Constitutional Convention, Lewis & Clark, etc. Every year it becomes more and more difficult to find young people who have any more than a passing acquaintance with these important events, let alone realize their significance. Book of Mormon prophets inspired the people by teaching the history of how their ancestors bore hardship and overcame evil, and we too need to make sure our youth know of the Americans who forged this free country out of the wilderness. If they are familiar with the events and principles that made America great, then they will be less likely to be persuaded by worldly ideologies and the unsound political philosophies of men.

Some Voting Criteria to Keep in Mind

Based on my studies of scripture and prophets, (both ancient and modern), the following are the basic criteria I keep in mind when deciding which candidates get my vote, and which legislation I support. I ask myself: "Is the candidate…?"

- A Constitutional Constructionist—This means that the Constitution is not seen as a "living" document that changes its meaning with society's whims, but is only amended through the means provided by the Constitution itself.
- Pro-life (today's PC rendition of anti-abortion)—The only exception I make to this criterion is when the office is smaller and really has no chance of making federal law or influencing abortion policy.
- Pro-Family—If the candidate supports any measures that weaken the family, then I do not vote for them. This could take many forms, from expanding the welfare state, to same-sex marriage, to laws that take responsibility from parents and transfer it to government.
- Anti-Drug/Gambling/Alcohol—We need candidates who will keep drugs illegal, oppose lotteries and maintain stiff penalties for drunk driving.
- Law and Order—There is a school of thought that criminals are created by society and punishment of criminals should be based on "rehabilitation." This is a faulty notion. Rehabilitation can certainly be part of criminal's punishment, but our justice system's principal role is to punish criminals, deter crime and otherwise protect the innocent and law-abiding.
- Keep taxes low—A government that expropriates from its citizens more money than is required to defend and protect life, liberty, and property rights, is violating its constitutional charter. (I still chuckle a little when I read the 19th chapter of Mosiah where the Lamanites enslaved and then taxed the people of King Limhi to the tune of 50%, and they called that taxation: "grievous to be born." We're taxed just about that much…by politicians we vote into office!)
- Balanced budget advocates—A small amount of debt relative to gross national product is not harmful, much like having a modest house and car

payment as a small portion of one's income Is not damaging; however, running large deficits has never been good for any economy.

There are of course other criteria that we need to consider; these points are simply patterns for our major areas of concern.

<u>The Family: A Proclamation to the World</u>—Political Ramifications

I anticipate that in the not too distant future, "The Proclamation on The Family" will be added to our canon of scripture. It is a magnificent revelation that, in a short eloquent series of paragraphs ties together most of the Gospel's plain and precious principles, while laying out God's will and plan for the family. Its principal thrust of course is to proclaim the importance of the family, the necessary conditions for preserving it, and to warn mankind of the consequences of failing to do so. It also carries some political ramification for Latter-day Saints, as well as for those who are not members of our church, and it behooves us to be anxiously engaged in seeing that its divine principles are woven into the unraveling fabric of our country's moral foundation.

"Gender is an essential characteristic…"

The proclamation's fourth sentence is of great importance in a day and age when Satan's forces are having growing success convincing people that gender is nothing more than circumstantial coincidence. If enough people believe that being a man or woman is a choice, as opposed to an unalterable part of who we are, one of the main foundational blocks of family building will have been torn away. Young people are being bombarded today with misguided ideas about transsexuals, bi-sexuals, transvestitism, the transgendered, and other ideas that twist gender into something that confuses them, instead of something that helps them to be happy. Most of these ideas used to be classified as mental illnesses by America's psychiatric health authorities…now they are simply lifestyle choices.

Another embattled idea in the proclamation is that **"…marriage between a man and a woman is essential to [God's] eternal plan."** There are myriad states trying to pass civil-union laws that would allow people of the same sex to marry. Efforts have been mounted to combat them, and thanks to the hard work of many people from many churches, most of these same sex laws have failed to pass. That does not mean the assaults will stop. The gay and lesbian lobbies have strong voices at all levels of government. The media and Hollywood are also part of the effort to convince people that these are "lifestyle choices" that are morally equivalent to marriage between a man and a woman.

We must be a chorus of strong, compassionate voices in favor of the family. Rants and other negative campaigning against homosexuality will not help us. A wise man once said that we won't persuade others to gather around our light by going around and snuffing out other's lights. We attract others to our light by making it shine brighter than all the rest. If we rely on the gentle urgings of the Spirit, together with our conviction of the principles in the Proclamation on the Family, the faithful will rally to Heaven's cause.

Parental vs. Government Accountability

> *"Parents have a sacred duty to rear their children in love and righteousness, to provide for their physical and spiritual needs...Husbands and wives—mothers and fathers—will be held accountable before God for the discharge of these obligations."*

One of the unfortunate effects of the welfare and entitlement mentality is that much of our society has come to believe that the government is the ultimate caretaker of America's children (and senior citizens). It was not like this for the first 175 years of America's history. During those years each family was the source of responsibility for its members, from youngest to oldest. Then the concept of a "safety net" was introduced, which is not a bad concept in and of itself, but unfortunately it has grown into something that harms as much or more than it helps. The harm came when the "safety net" became detached from the family and grew into a welfare state that rewarded single parenthood, instead of being a vehicle for helping families get back on their feet as originally intended. This slow change in the personal responsibility mindset has resulted in the following types of comments on societal misfortune: *"the government will take care of them,"* or *"the system failed her."* This kind of thinking has turned many in our nation into people who look to the government, instead of to themselves and family, for the basic necessities of life. This in turn has produced elections that turn on taking something from someone and giving it to someone else. No wonder the electorate is "divided!" It behooves us to follow the prophet and call on our government leaders to re-orient our nation's charitable institutions toward the family, and oppose the creation and expansion of entitlement programs.

"We call upon responsible citizens and officers of government everywhere…"

The Proclamation on the Family is directed to the entire world, yet the brethren saw fit to emphasize a certain segment of the world in the last paragraph. They call upon citizens and government officials everywhere to promote the principles of the proclamation in order to strengthen the world's families. Since not all responsible citizens and government officers will read the proclamation otherwise, we can help by following the example of our church leaders by presenting the proclamation to our elected officials, community leaders and any others that the spirit might lead us to share it with.

I have included portions of the proclamation in emails and letters to elected officials. It does not hurt our cause to share the proclamation and then communicate to our leaders that there are millions of our church, (currently the fifth largest in the United States), that share these ideals. If we rally around the principles of the Proclamation on the Family and present a united voice of responsible Latter-day Saint citizens, we will become an indispensable vote to court when politicians are campaigning, forming policy, writing legislation, and otherwise shaping America's destiny.

"Of One Heart and One Mind"

Becoming a Zion people means that we will become of one heart and one mind. This not only refers to things spiritual, but applies to the political also. Since the Gospel only flourishes in free political systems, championing righteous political principles is a vital part of our spiritual citizenship. As President John Taylor said about things political, *"let us be one and operate as one, for God and his kingdom."* Bruce R. McConkie urged the Saints to unity in all things:

> *If we, as a people, keep the commandments of God; if we take the side of the Church on all issues,* **both religious and political***; if we take the Holy Spirit for our guide; if we give heed to the words of the apostles and prophets who minister among us—then, from an eternal standpoint, all things will work together for our good.*
> Elder Bruce R. McConkie, Ensign, November, 1980, p.73 (bold, author's)

We live in the latter days, when sides are being chosen. The hymn "Who's on the Lord's Side?" says it better than I can:

> The powers of earth and hell in rage direct the blow.
> That's aimed to crush the work; Who's on the Lord's side? Who?

Truth, life, and liberty, freedom from death and woe,
Are stakes we're fighting for; Who's on the Lord's side? Who?
Who's on the Lord's side? Who? Now is the time to show.
We ask it fearlessly: Who's on the Lord's side? Who?
Hymns #260, verse 4

    I hope that we, as a unified people in the Stakes of Zion everywhere, will take the instructions and teachings we have received from the brethren and then go to the ballot box with a determination to take the Lord's side in all things.

Chapter 6

Befriending the Constitution = Conserving the Constitution

- Are Latter-day Saints Liberals or Conservatives?
- Definitions of "Liberal" and "Conservative"
- Befriending & Conserving the First Amendment to the Constitution
- Ezra Taft Benson:
  - Befriender of the Constitution
  - Never Backed Down in His Support of Freedom
  - Prophetic in the Political
  - Friend to God and to the Constitution
- How Can We Befriend the Constitution?

Are Latter-day Saints Liberals or Conservatives?

Sometimes people ask me if a faithful Latter-day Saint should be of the liberal or conservative philosophy, or if we belong with the republicans or the democrats, (or libertarians or independents.) I reply that the Latter-day Saints do indeed have a political philosophy but that it is based on *Gospel principles as opposed to party politics*. Those principles are found throughout the scriptures and the Constitution of the United States of America, as well as other inspired founding documents such as the Declaration of Independence and the Federalist Papers.

Shortly before Pearl Harbor was bombed, President J. Reuben Clark said the following from the pulpit at General Conference:

> *"In this country our lawful political allegiance runs not to any man, not to any party, not to any "ism," but to the Constitution of the United States and to the free institutions set up under it. There can be no tampering with the "just and holy principles" of the Constitution. No true Latter-day Saint can or will do other than reverence the Constitution; each will do all in his power to save it from pollution or destruction."*
>
> J. Reuben Clark, Jr., Conference Report, April 1941, p.19

Since we have been commanded to "befriend...the constitutional law of the land," the answer to the question is twofold:

> 1—Our first political loyalty, and thus our vote, is for the "just and holy" principles of the Constitution...regardless of party tag.
>
> 2—Because our charge is to conserve the Constitution, (and the brethren have informed us that the Constitution is under attack), that makes Latter-day Saints conservatives.

Caveat

In saying that Latter-day Saints are conservatives, I am not saying that there is some sort of spiritual mandate to be members of the party most commonly associated with the word "conservative." Though the case may be made that of the two major parties in existence today, the Republican party's platform is the one most favorable to conserving the Constitution, <u>no</u> party has a monopoly on preserving and protecting the Constitution. I am a republican and a conservative, but that is secondary to my devotion to the Gospel; if I had been born earlier in the last century, I might well have belonged to a different political party. I advocate that all members be actively engaged in preserving the just and holy principles found in the Constitution of the United States of America…**no matter which party they belong to.**

Definitions of "Liberal" and "Conservative"

These two words are often misused and/or misunderstood in today's political dialogue because their definitions have shifted over the years. "Conservative" and "liberal" are not two well-defined political positions that always mean the same thing. They only define someone's political views *as they relate to another political position.*

Liberal

The basic definition of a liberal is someone who favors progress or reform of the government in which they are currently living. Liberalism also connotes giving the individual more liberty (which is the root of the word liberal), as opposed to more government control over its citizens. A good example would be the framers of the Constitution. The founding fathers were correctly labeled liberals because they advocated a democratically elected, limited government with greater individual rights of representation, freedom and property, as opposed to the royal monarchy in which they were living. (That was 1776 though. If the founding fathers were alive today they would most certainly be labeled conservatives.)

After the American Revolution however, the term 'liberal' held little meaning until around the time of Franklin Delano Roosevelt's presidency during the Great Depression. The enacting of large government programs advocated by FDR as a response to the depression was really the beginning of the creation of the two sides of the political debate we have today. In our current political configuration, liberals are associated with beliefs such as increased government intervention, higher taxes, unlimited abortion rights, an expanding welfare state, and race-based preferences. Thus the original definition of liberalism has been turned on its head as today's liberals advocate higher taxes and more government involvement in everyday life.

Elder Neal A. Maxwell describes how difficult it will be to remedy the effects of this new liberalism that grew the government exponentially after FDR's presidency:

> "It remains to be seen whether or not our nation can tame big government. There is, frankly, no precedent for dismantling, even partially, a welfare state, especially in a peaceful and constitutional way. Such a Goliath will not go quietly to surgery…
> We are experiencing these symptoms in America. Yet, alas, Thomas Jefferson said

our republic's future rested on the assumption that our citizens would remain attentive and informed."

(The original text of the Jefferson quote Elder Maxwell refers to is one of my favorites: "If a nation expects to be ignorant and free...it expects what never was and never will be." Or as I have paraphrased it: If a nation expects to be ignorant and free, it will end up with plenty of the former and none of the latter!) Elder Maxwell continues:

"The shift in values has produced another shift in political point of view. George F. Will, the perceptive Pulitzer Prize-winning columnist, noted just one example in the difference between the old liberalism and a new liberalism:

"The old liberalism delivered material advantages that were intended to enable people to live the lives they had chosen. The new liberalism, typified by forced busing and affirmative action and the explosive growth of regulation, administers 'remedies' to what society's supervisors consider defects in the way people live." *(Newsweek, 23 Jan. 1978, p. 88)*

Decrease the belief in God, and you increase the numbers of those who wish to play at being God by being "society's supervisors." Such "supervisors" deny the existence of divine standards, but are very serious about imposing their own standards on society."

Elder Neal A Maxwell, "The Prohibitive Costs of a Value-Free Society," Ensign, October 1978 (bold, author's)

Elder Maxwell describes the battleground between liberal and conservative in today's political arena with his usual flair. The liberalism of the founding fathers was a liberalism of freedom; the liberalism of today is one where only elites are free to dictate how the rest should live their lives.

Conservative

If you are a conservative, it means that you want to conserve the original form of government. (In 1776 being conservative meant that you were on the side of the British because you wanted to conserve the existing government.) In today's political scene, being conservative means that you are trying to conserve the constitutional republic of limited federal government left to us by the founding fathers. A conservative today is for strong defense, narrow government involvement in our lives, non-progressive taxation, and reducing the size and scope of government assistance programs. This has become a very tall order in an age when many feel that the government (i.e., their fellow citizens) "owes" them an education, a job, or some other kind of subsistence.

Benjamin Franklin knew that maintaining a constitutional republic would be a huge undertaking when he signed the Constitution. As Franklin was leaving Independence Hall, a Mrs. Powel of Philadelphia asked the great statesman:

> *"Well, Doctor, what have we got, a republic or a monarchy?"*
> *Without the slightest hesitation, Franklin responded:*
> *"A republic, if you can keep it."*

Since the time of FDR, conservatives have been associated with conserving and preserving the limited, constitutional government the founders left us. Although some correct constitutional government policies can be found in most of the current political organizations, of the two major parties, the Republican Party is home to the greatest number of constitutionally conservative positions.

Befriending & Conserving the First Amendment to the Constitution

> *"Congress shall make no law respecting an establishment of religion, or prohibiting the free exercise thereof; or abridging the freedom of speech, or of the press; or the right of the people peaceably to assemble, and to petition the government for a redress of grievances."*
> 1st Amendment to the U.S. Constitution

In Doctrine and Covenants section 134, verse 2, it says:
"We believe that no government can exist in peace, except such laws are framed and held inviolate as will secure to each individual the free exercise of conscience…"
Freedom of religion is one of the greatest cornerstones of the Constitution as well as the essence of what the war in heaven was fought over. This precious freedom is under attack. President James E. Faust, in a speech at Utah State University on Sept. 16, 2001 described the danger (Pres. Faust prefaced his talks by saying that he was speaking only on his own account and his remarks were his opinion only):

> *"The preeminence in the Constitution of the free exercise clause of the First Amendment has been overshadowed by the establishment clause and the free speech clause. In this I believe there has been a turning away from the intent of the Founding Fathers in the Supreme Court's interpretation of these clauses of the First Amendment."*

President Faust then summed up the essence of the problem of how congress and the courts were encroaching upon churches' free exercise of religion:

> *"There seems to be developing a new secular creed. It has no moral absolutes. It is non-denominational. It is non-theistic. It is politically focused. It is antagonistic to religion. It rejects the historic religious traditions of this nation. It feels strange. If this trend continues, non-belief will be more honored than belief. While all beliefs must be protected, are atheism, agnosticism, cynicism and moral relativism to be more safeguarded and valued than Christianity, Judaism and the tenets of Islam which hold that there is a Supreme Being and that mortals are accountable to him? If so, this would, in my opinion, place this nation in great moral jeopardy."*

I believe President Faust's conclusions hit the nail right on the head. The United States congress and judiciary are heading farther and farther away from the recognition that God-fearing men created this nation and that the Constitution will only function, as President John Adams said, for "a moral and religious people." James Madison, regarded by historians as "The Father of the Constitution" said:

> *"Before any man can be considered as a member of civil society, he must be considered as a subject of the Governor of the Universe, religion (is) the basis and foundation of government."*
> James Madison, "Memorial and Remonstrance" To the Honorable the General Assembly of the Commonwealth of Virginia

Another Madison quote is instructive:

> "It is the mutual duty of all to practice Christian forbearance, love and charity toward each other." Virginia Declaration of Rights, 1776

Ezra Taft Benson—Befriender of the Constitution

President Benson was a great defender of the Constitution. His professional, religious, and political activities consistently honored the just and holy principles upon which the United States of America was founded. As President Dwight D. Eisenhower's Secretary of Agriculture, he worked tirelessly to eliminate the farm subsidy programs created during the depression that had outlived their usefulness. As an apostle and prophet he taught the Constitution from the pulpit with staunch eloquence.

Elder Benson was called to be an apostle in 1943; nine years later he was nominated by president Dwight D. Eisenhower to become his Secretary of Agriculture. Elder Benson was reluctant to accept the nomination for fear of mixing church and politics, but changed his mind and accepted the post after being urged to do so by the president of the church at that time—David O. McKay.

The trio of Elder Benson, President McKay, and counselor in the first presidency, J. Reuben Clark, became one of the clearest and most forceful voices for righteous political involvement the church has ever seen. Ezra Benson's main contribution in political life was his unflinching stand against socialist farm practices that had been instituted during the New Deal years of the Depression. After accepting the nomination, in his "General Statement on Agricultural Policy" he said "A completely planned and subsidized economy weakens initiative, discourages industry, destroys character, and demoralizes the people." From there Secretary Benson fought hard for the reduction and elimination of farm subsidies, price fixing, and other welfare-state policies, but had only limited success. He might have been more successful if not for the strong voices of farm welfare policies in both Congress and the Department of Agriculture. (It's an interesting historical note that the first major Communist cell exposed in Washington, the Ware Cell—which included the notorious perjurer Alger Hiss—was entrenched in the Department of Agriculture.)

As a step in the right direction, Secretary Benson fought hard for the replacement of rigid price supports with a flexible-support system. The latter, he believed, while far from ideal, would at least alleviate some market distortions that nearly 20 years of government interference in agriculture had created. While still unconstitutional, flexible supports were at least a step in the right direction.

Ezra Benson Never Backed Down in His Support of Freedom

In 1959, Communist dictator Premier Nikita Khrushchev made a visit to the United States. After being asked by President Eisenhower, Secretary Benson agreed with extreme reluctance to accompany Khrushchev and his entourage on a tour of a USDA station. "My enthusiasm for the project," he later recorded, "could have been put in a small thimble...," nevertheless, he made the most of the occasion. At one point during Khrushchev's visit, the Soviet Premier boasted to Ezra Benson that his own grandchildren would one day live under Communism. (Those old enough to remember will identify this as the same boast Khrushchev made from the floor of the U.N. on that memorable day when the Soviet dictator pounded his shoe on the table.) Benson replied to the dictator's face that he expected to do all in his power to assure that Khrushchev's and all other grandchildren would live under freedom. The Communist leader then responded, according to Benson's personal account: "You Americans are so gullible. No, you won't accept communism outright, but we'll keep feeding you small doses of socialism until you'll finally wake up and find you already have communism." Thanks to President Benson and many other staunch cold warriors, the grandchildren of both men are not living under Nikita Khrushchev's foolhardy prediction, but according to Ezra Taft Benson's pledge.

Prophetic in the Political

In hindsight, Ezra Taft Benson's wisdom as Secretary of Agriculture is irrefutable. Liberals persuaded voters that farm subsidies would benefit the "family farmer" and keep them from being wiped out by large corporate farming interests. Secretary Benson opposed farm subsidies, saying: "You can't run the nation's farms from behind a desk in Washington." He maintained that subsidies would hurt the small farmer and fought for the reduction and eventual elimination of farm subsidies.

Benson turned out to be right. Today, the entrance barrier in money and regulations for one man to become a farmer is enormous…virtually impossible to accomplish. And while politicians love to discuss the plight of the small farmer, they actually dole out the bulk of the subsidies to the largest farms and corporations. In 2002, the top 10 percent of farmers collected 65 percent of total subsidies, a share worth $7.8 billion. And who received most of those taxpayer dollars?…not family farmers. The top recipients were corporate farming companies, banks, Indian tribes, and land management companies. Subsidies also work against their own stated goal, by creating a never-ending cycle of dependence: farmers demand subsidies because of low market prices for their products, while those same subsidies keep prices low instead of letting them respond to the normal market forces of supply and demand.

Ezra Taft Benson—Friend to God and to the Constitution

President Benson was always a missionary for political freedom while working in his church calling, (note his many quotes from the pulpit in chapter 4), and he was always a missionary for the Gospel while working at his political job. A few weeks after Khrushchev's visit to the United States, Secretary Benson visited the Soviet Union. The moment he arrived he started asking his hosts to take him to one of Moscow's Protestant Church services, but was repeatedly rebuffed. On the last night of his visit, he made one final attempt. While being driven through the pouring rain to the airport, he mentioned to his guide that he was disappointed not to have been able to attend a Christian worship service. His guide barked an order to the chauffeur, and the car abruptly turned into a side street to the Central Baptist Church, not too far from Red Square.

Contrary to what Elder Benson had been led to believe, the church was filled with worshippers of all ages. A newsman who was there described what happened as Ezra Benson and his entourage were led to the front of the church and seated beside the pulpit: "Every face in the old sanctuary gaped incredulously as our obviously American group was led down the aisle…They reached out to touch us almost as one would reach out for the final last caress of one's most beloved just before the casket is lowered. They were in misery and yet a light shone through the misery. They gripped our hands like frightened children."

To Benson's surprise, the minister asked him to speak to the congregation. Elder Benson then greeted the Russian Christians on behalf of "millions and millions of church people in America and around the world. He testified: "God lives, I know that he lives…Jesus Christ, the Redeemer of the World watches over this earth…Be unafraid, keep His commandments, love one another, pray for peace and all will be well." Elder Benson also spoke on the power of prayer, the reality of eternity and the resurrection. He concluded with the following witness, that: "the truth will endure. Time is on the side of truth."

As Elder Benson and those that were with him left the warmth of the church and went out into the rain-soaked night, the congregation sang the familiar hymn, "God Be With You Till We Meet Again." The American press corps in Benson's entourage, who had witnessed the scene, were especially moved. Even the most cynical among them wept openly. Grant Salisbury wrote in U.S. News & World Report: "It turned out to be one of the most moving experiences in the lifetime of many of us. One newsman…ranked it with the sight of the American flag rising over the old American compound in Tientsin, China, at the end of World War II." Another recorded: "Imagine getting your greatest spiritual experience in atheistic Russia…It was the most heart-rending and most inspiring scene I've ever witnessed." As Secretary Benson and his entourage quietly boarded their waiting cars, one of the reporters summed up the entire episode: "I believe they were the only really happy people we saw in Russia."

Ezra Taft Benson served God and befriended the Constitution in virtually every aspect of his religious and professional life. Though many disagreed with him, nobody ever doubted his devotion to both God and country.

How can we "befriend" the Constitution?

I've often thought about the Lord's use of the word "befriend" in the 98th section of the Doctrine and Covenants. Why didn't he use a word like 'obey', 'honor', 'defend' that we normally hear used when talking about these kinds of documents? I think it's because 'befriend' conveys not only obedience and honor, but befriend, (or "be a friend"), also includes the aspect of affection or charity. Now that doesn't mean that we should have affection for a document on a piece of paper, but it does mean that we should love the principles therein. After all, we are conservatives working to conserve the U.S. Constitution not because we seek power to rule over others, but because we seek freedom for our neighbors, as well as those all over the world. Befriending the Constitution means that we actively promote its principles among those who are laboring under Satan's plan of force as we invite them to taste the Gospel of freedom. I believe that befriending the Constitution also means that our domestic political efforts should be concentrated on defending it from its enemies in our own country who are chipping away at the Constitution's foundations and principles, and thus are chipping away at our moral agency.

Chapter 7

Recognizing Attacks on the Constitution

- **Beware of Attacks on Motives as Opposed to Actions**
- **Pre-Labeling—Another Way the Opposition Attacks Motive**
- **Right-Wing Extremists, (Tigers and Bears, Oh My!)**
- **Reliance on "The Arm of Flesh"—Secular & Worldly Knowledge**
- **They Make It Complicated and Complex**
- **Changing the Terms of the Debate**
- **Moral Relativism (Everyone's Doing It)**
- **Politically Timed Attacks**
- **Flaxen Cords**

Those who befriend the Constitution will be opposed by those who do not believe in its principles; they say they do, but they have no desire to preserve its just and holy principles. These forces are constantly engaged in undercutting its foundations a little at a time. These patient incrementalists work bit by bit to tear at the individual fibers of that great document. The Apostle Paul described this ongoing struggle:

> *"For we wrestle not against flesh and blood, but against principalities, against powers, against the rulers of the darkness of this world, against spiritual wickedness in high places."* (Ephesians 6:12)

A principality is defined as: "a state ruled by a prince, usually a relatively small state or a state that falls within a larger state such as an empire." So in Paul's scenario, Satan is a powerful prince, (but not more powerful than the king), and he sets up his "principalities" or mini-kingdoms of spiritual wickedness and darkness and then he and his angels attack and withdraw. The same tactic is used on the political battlefield. Those who advocate the constitution's slow decay and eventual destruction know that they can't come out and state their true aim, so they attack key laws and policies from their bureaucratic and political strongholds, and then withdraw. It's important that we're able to recognize the efforts of the Constitution's enemies so we can combat them with our vote and by withholding our political support. This chapter's purpose is to highlight the subtle tactics used by the opponents of the Constitution so we can recognize the enemy's influence immediately and not be fooled by his subtlety.

Beware of Attacks on Motives as Opposed to Actions

> *And he (Korihor) did rise up in great swelling words before Alma, and did revile against the priests and teachers, accusing them of leading away the people after the silly traditions of their fathers, for the sake of glutting on the labors of the people.* (Alma 30: 31)

As we observe the political discourse of our day we need to hear both sides of every issue. American democracy is founded upon the concept of "the loyal opposition." Our history is sprinkled with great debates on the important issues of the day. Disagreement is to be expected, as it is perfectly reasonable that good and well-meaning people will disagree on any number of topics. However, it's vital that we are able to distinguish a reasoned argument from one designed to direct attention away from the specifics of the opposition's point of view by attacking the opponent. This scripture from Alma is a perfect example of an attack on motive as opposed to actions and ideas.

No one can truly know another person's reasons and motives are with 100% certainty, but it feeds a certain type of person's ego to think so…which is why the opposition loves this type of attack. Once someone can be convinced that another person means them harm, or desires to hurt one segment of the population, no rational argument will have an effect on that person. If someone accuses person X of wanting to harm person Y, how can person X respond, other than to say that it's not true? There is no way to respond verbally; the only recourse for person X is to let his actions show that he means no harm to person Y. Unfortunately in the political arena, that takes time and it also takes effort on the part of the listening and watchful citizen to actually take into account what person X actually does, instead of listen to accusations about him. When listening to political discourse or reading about the issues of the day we need to recognize accusations based on someone's supposed knowledge of someone else's motives or desires.

Examples of Attacks on Motive/Intent

Here are a few common examples where the technique is casting shadows on personal motives instead of concentrating on political substance:

"They're coming for our children, they're coming for the poor, they're coming for the sick, the elderly, and the disabled."
—Congressman John Lewis-D, Georgia, speech on House floor opposing the 1995 Republican welfare reform bill, March 21, 1995

"...the...Ku Klux Klan members worked to improve race relations: They, too, reached out to blacks with nooses and burning crosses."
Representative William Clay-D, Missouri on George W. Bush's selection of John Ashcroft as Attorney General
(Steve Benson, syndicated editorial cartoonist, depicted Ashcroft wearing white robes and enthusiastically brandishing a noose as Bush restrains him: "Easy, John—I said your confirmation should be a cinch—a cinch.")

"Pittsburgh is going to say no to the NRA, no to its policies which promote violence, and no to the hate the NRA leadership spreads...The NRA will go to any length to increase the culture of fear in the United States in order to create a broader market for the gun industry's products...Under the guise of the Second Amendment and traditional American family values, the NRA promotes white patriarchal culture—straight white Christian men defending America against the onslaught of alien others. NRA leaders explicitly fan the flames of bigotry..."
—Nathaniel Glosser, Press Release from "Confluence Against Gun Violence", April 8, 2004, opposing the National Rifle Association (NRA) lead-

ership and its annual convention, which was to be held in Pittsburgh on April 16–18.

"Something got screwed up in terms of your priorities if you think it's more important to get rid of the dividend tax than it is to take care of 11 million kids."
—Washington Post's David Broder on NBC's Meet the Press, June 1, 2003.

"The new Republican majority in Congress took a big step today on its legislative agenda to demolish or damage government aid programs, many of them designed to help children and the poor."
—Dan Rather on CBS Evening News, March 16, 1995

Notice how these statements do not attack policies or public actions, but supposed ill intentions possessed by others. A good example of how this tactic was exposed and successfully refuted is found in Ronald Reagan's seminal 1964 speech "A Time For Choosing":

"Any time you and I question the schemes of the do-gooders, we're denounced as being opposed to their humanitarian goals. It seems impossible to legitimately debate their solutions with the assumption that all of us share the desire to help the less fortunate."

At that time, Republicans were trying to reform the Social Security program because it was running out of money. Democrats did not respond to that simple accounting deficiency with any kind of substantive solution, instead, they merely attacked the reformers by telling the public that conservatives' real aim was to "starve the elderly." Reagan did not let the opposition's attack on his compassion intimidate him. He identified their faulty accusation and refuted it:

"We are for a provision that destitution should not follow unemployment by reason of old age, and to that end we have accepted Social Security as a step toward meeting the problem. However, we are against those entrusted with this program when they practice deception regarding its fiscal shortcomings, when they charge that any criticism of the program means that we want to end payments."

The tactics of the Constitution's enemies in this regard have not changed, and this is one of the most important tricks to look out for as we listen to all political voices—candidates, media, party spokesmen, etc:

One of the greatest political tricks is to change questions of _fact_ into accusations of _motive or intent_.

Pre-Labeling—Another Way the Opposition Attacks Motive

> *Brother Jacob, I have sought much opportunity that I might speak unto you; for I...know that thou goest about much, preaching that which ye call the gospel, or the doctrine of Christ.*
> *And ye have led away much of this people that they pervert the right way of God, and keep not the law of Moses which is the right way; and convert the law of Moses into the worship of a being which ye say shall come many hundred years hence. (Jacob 7:6–7)*

The opposition knows that if one side's ideas can be pre-labeled in such a way that they lose credibility from the start, others probably won't give the ideas a fair hearing. Labeling people, groups, or ideas as being "anti" or "unfriendly" to something conventionally perceived as good, is just another way to attack motives as opposed to substance.

Here's a good example from the mainstream media of a "pre-labeled" idea, designed to encourage people to tune out before they actually hear the idea:

> *"Next week on ABC's World News Tonight, a series of reports about our environment which will tell you precisely what the new Congress has in mind: the most frontal assault on the environment in 25 years. Is this what the country wants? On ABC's World News Tonight next week."*
> —Peter Jennings, ABC promo, July 9, 1995 "This Week with David Brinkley"

Note that Mr. Jennings promotes the story not by telling anything about the legislation; he just labels it an assault on the environment. I don't believe that anybody in any kind of a position of power, be they democrat, republican, libertarian or independent wishes to assault the environment. That promo makes that assumption though. Imagine if a politician wanted to re-introduce optional prayer in public school, (something Latter-day Saints would certainly endorse), but the idea was introduced as "an assault on public education." It would be very hard to get a hearing on the initiative, (and that's the way the enemy wants it!)

Government actions that constitutional conservatives support have had the following labels applied to them: "mean-spirited," "selfish," "extreme Christian right," and "hateful," or "hate speech." This is one of the principal ways that Satan lulls people into inactivity or gets them to oppose righteous ends—he distorts those ends and makes them appear to be something other than what they really are. We are currently witnessing the fulfillment of Isaiah's prophecy:

Wo unto them that call evil good, and good evil, that put darkness for light, and light for darkness, that put bitter for sweet, and sweet for bitter!
(2 Nephi 15:20)

Right-Wing Extremists, (Tigers and Bears, Oh My!)

This is one of the opposition's favorite terms to describe constitutional conservatives. Here's a short checklist to determine whether today's opponents of the Constitution would call you a "right-wing extremist":

- Do you favor limited constitutional government with specific enumerated powers given to those who govern us?
- Are you against ever-expanding welfare state and entitlement growth?
- Are you anti-abortion?
- Do you think the phrase "under God" in the pledge of allegiance is constitutional?

If you answered "yes" to any of the questions above, you're considered a right wing extremist by today's media. The big problem with the word "extreme" is that those who use the term never define the ends of the scale that mark the two extremes. In order to be an extremist, the middle as well as both extremes needs to be understood by all. The United States of America has had a sliding scale of political left and right extremes that has been changing ever since 1776. 200 years ago, if you had come up with a Social Security program as Roosevelt did, you would have been ignored as crazy or laughed at for completely misunderstanding the Constitution. 100 years ago, if you advocated a Social Security System, you would have been called an extreme left wing socialist radical. Today, if you simply want to reform the Social Security so it doesn't go bankrupt after the baby boomers retire, you're a right wing radical. See how the extremes change over the years?

The true right wing extremists today are found in the separatist, doomsday, polygamy, or 'abolish-the-government' type groups. The mainstream media has labeled Ronald Reagan, and both Presidents Bush as extreme right-wingers when in fact they were nowhere near the rightward extreme of the political spectrum. Whenever you hear someone called an extremist, find out what that person considers extreme first; chances are, they're not. The same applies to liberals. Bill

Clinton, who was portrayed as an extreme leftist, was really not. Though he did hold some very liberal positions, he also signed welfare reform, NAFTA, and several other bills that were very much supported from the republican side of the aisle. Beware of the label "extreme" when applied to someone at the national level; it rarely applies since it's very difficult to get more than 50% of the entire country to elect a true extremist. Labeling someone an extremist is also just a lazy way of attacking someone; we would be wise to ignore the term.

Reliance on "The Arm of Flesh"—Secular & Worldly Knowledge

> O that cunning plan of the evil one! O the vainness, and the frailties, and the foolishness of men! When they are learned they think they are wise, and they hearken not unto the counsel of God, for they set it aside, supposing they know of themselves, wherefore, their wisdom is foolishness and it profiteth them not. And they shall perish. (2 Nephi 9: 28)

The elevation of worldly learning and knowledge over God's wisdom and humility is always popular with the opposition. One of the first things that gets said about politicians who are plain-spoken, and who label evil as evil, is that they are mentally challenged. This is just another way of attacking someone personally instead of dealing with the substance of their positions. We have a couple of stellar examples of this in recent history.

One of the renowned intellectuals of the 70's and 80's, Clark Clifford, labeled Ronald Reagan, an "amiable dunce." Now no matter what one thinks of President Reagan's political actions, it is impossible that he was a fool who just lucked into the office. No one on luck alone gets elected governor of the largest state in the country twice, then comes within a whisker of wresting the Republican party nomination from a sitting president, and then goes on to win two terms as president of the United States. Reagan was successful and his opponents hated him and called him stupid because he was willing to apply moral labels instead of clouding his speech with pseudo-intellectual jargon. When he labeled the Soviet Union "an evil empire," the communist sympathizers in the U.S. came unglued. Not just because they disagreed, but because Reagan was willing to say it out loud with the force of conviction and then let the people decide whether or not they agreed or not.

Today many in the media and intellectual circles freely label George W. Bush as a simpleton, (even though he has a Harvard M.B.A.!), simply because he has a Texas accent, or can't pronounce some words well. He too, is willing to use plain terms such as "Axis of Evil" and then let the American people decide whether or not they agree.

We must disregard personal attacks in the form of insults to someone's intellect when making decisions about which candidates to vote for. Learning is wonderful and we believe that "the glory of God is intelligence" (D&C 93:36), but it is not the lynchpin upon which we make decisions about people. Character, integrity, honesty and a host of other virtues need to accompany worldly learning in order to make righteous decisions in the governing of others. Name calling is also an ugly form of campaigning and we should shun those who employ it.

They Make It Complicated and Complex

The Savior condemned those who complicated the Law of Moses:

> *For God commanded, saying, Honour thy father and mother: and, He that curseth father or mother, let him die the death.*
> *But ye say, Whosoever shall say to his father or his mother, It is a gift, by whatsoever thou mightest be profited by me;*
> *And honour not his father or his mother, he shall be free. Thus have ye made the commandment of God of none effect by your tradition.* (Matthew 15:4–6)

One of the biggest successes Satan had in ancient Israel was the perverting of Mosaic Law by sects like the Pharisees and Sadducees. They took that plain and simple law and added many variations and traditions to it, thus making it one of the largest and most complex legal systems known to man at the time. Then they set themselves up as the sole interpreters of those myriad tradition-laws, and the Jews ended up with a law that was not just and which the average citizen did not understand. We're witnessing the same phenomenon today.

One of the biggest hurdles to being politically well informed is because of the massive complexity that has come with big government that has grown beyond its constitutional limits. Just get a copy of the federal budget if you want to be overwhelmed. Or try reading the United States Code. We all have spent many hours just trying to figure out the tax code alone! Someone once said that when this country's laws had grown so massive and complex that a man of average education could not comprehend them, then we would know that our system of justice is doomed. We are currently awash in a mass of laws, statutes, regulations, codes that would make the Pharisee's version of Mosaic Law look small by comparison.

Be wary of legislation and policy that cannot be explained easily or written down in a comprehensible fashion. The devil is usually in the details.

Changing the Terms of the Debate

> *"It simply is not true that our private conduct is our own business. Our society is the sum total of what millions of individuals do in their private lives. That sum total of private behavior has worldwide public consequences of enormous magnitude. There are no completely private choices."*
> Elder James E. Faust, "Will I Be Happy?" Ensign, May 1987

> *"The woman's choice for her own body does not validate choice for the body of another. The expression "terminate the pregnancy" applies literally only to the woman. The consequence of terminating the fetus therein involves the body and very life of another. These two individuals have separate brains, separate hearts, and separate circulatory systems. To pretend that there is no child and no life there is to deny reality."*
> Elder Russell M. Nelson, "Reverence for Life" Ensign, May 1985

Another technique to continually be on the alert for is the changing of the terms of debate by introducing new words for things that do not need a new word. Abortion is the best example. Pro-abortion advocates needed to change the focus away from the killing of an unborn child to something more sympathetically viewed by the public—women's rights. Thus the concept of "choice" was born. This has worked well for the pro-abortion advocates because who can be against someone else's freedom and choice? Changing the terms of debate is one of the ways Satan has succeeded in getting the American people's sanction for killing millions of their fellow-citizens.

Moral Relativism (Everyone's Doing It)

> *Yea, and there shall be many which shall say: Eat, drink, and be merry, for tomorrow we die; and it shall be well with us. (2 Nephi 28: 7)*

"Everyone else is doing it" has long been one of Satan's most useful tactics for making people miserable. The world of politics has its own brand called "moral relativism." Moral relativism is the theory that morality, or standards of right and wrong, are culturally based and therefore are a matter of individual choice. Elder Dallin Oaks gives us the proper direction regarding this errant philosophy:

> *"One of the consequences of shifting from moral absolutes to moral relativism in public policy is that this produces a corresponding shift of emphasis from responsi-*

bilities to rights. Responsibilities originate in moral absolutes. In contrast, rights find their origin in legal principles, which are easily manipulated by moral relativism.

In the United States, the moral absolutes are the ones derived from what we refer to as the Judeo-Christian tradition, as set forth in the Bible—Old Testament and New Testament.

Despite ample evidence of majority adherence to moral absolutes, some still question the legitimacy of a moral foundation for our laws and public policy. To avoid any suggestion of adopting or contradicting any particular religious absolute, some secularists argue that our laws must be entirely neutral, with no discernable relation to any particular religious tradition. Such proposed neutrality is unrealistic, unless we are willing to cut away the entire idea that there are moral absolutes."

Dallin H. Oaks, "Religious Values and Public Policy," Ensign, Oct. 1992

Moral relativism also encompasses those who try to excuse their behavior by trying to cite the behavior of others as a rationalization for it. One of the most disturbing legacies of the Clinton administration is the extent to which America has embraced the idea of moral relativism. Many Americans today believe that there are now two moralities, a personal one and a social one, and the former is somehow less important than the latter. By this definition, the morality of an individual's action is irrelevant as long as it is judged (don't ask by whom) to be serving a greater public good. When Bill Clinton made welcome and unwelcome sexual advances, and then viciously slandered the women who reported his behavior—the very people who had once found such actions morally reprehensible, suddenly found them completely normal. ("Everyone lies about sex.")

We cannot allow the plain and precious truths of the Gospel to be "deconstructed" so that evil can be excused, and good people and principles made into evil things. The teachings of Christ will be an anchor for us as we wade through the moral relativism of today's political rhetoric.

Politically Timed Attacks

We should always take care to make sure we uphold honorable and wise men. Unfortunately, in these latter days, Americans have not made honor and morality a premier requirement in electing public officials. There is also the improbability that those we elect have led perfect lives before running for office. Many times we will have to pull the lever in favor of people that do not uphold or practice *everything* we believe.

Of course we as voters need to examine all the pertinent circumstances of a candidates' past decisions. We also need to be on the lookout that we do not let politically timed media attacks eliminate good candidates who have changed their lives and are now honestly trying to uphold the Constitution.

Politically timed attacks are another form of media bias, but I thought it belonged in this chapter because although the media is complicit, it is mostly one side of the political spectrum that spearheads the effort:

Breaking Scandals Right Before An Election
Be on the lookout the week before an election. It's an ideal time for a politically timed attack because:

A. It's usually sensationalistic and people generally take more notice of scandal than substance.

B. The candidate attacked is forced to use the last precious 4 or 5 days of a campaign defending themselves, instead of using that time to drive their message home to people who are in the process of making up their minds.

Two examples:

- The Thursday before the October 2003 gubernatorial recall election, the Los Angeles Times ran a story on Arnold Schwarzenegger where 6 women (only two of whom would go on the record) accused Mr. Schwarzenegger of unwanted sexual advances. (I am in no way advocating that Mr. Schwarzenegger should not be scrutinized for his behavior. However, the fact that no one prosecuted him over all those years, and that it just *happened* to come out the week before the election should make the accusations suspect)

- The week preceding the 2000 presidential election, a news reporter in Maine breaks a story on a 24-year-old drunk driving charge against George W. Bush that originated with a lawyer who had served as a Democratic National Convention delegate.

These types of attacks also occur in state and local elections. These are just the most notable examples. Again, I am not attempting to excuse sexual harassment or drunk driving; what I am saying is that the opposition's tactics tell you just as much about their character and fitness for office as another candidate's past.

Flaxen Cords

> *And there are also secret combinations, even as in times of old, according to the combinations of the devil, for he is the founder of all these things; yea, the founder of murder, and works of darkness; yea, and he leadeth them by the neck with a flaxen cord, until he bindeth them with his strong cords forever.* (2 Nephi 26: 22)

These are just a few of the most popular techniques of those who try to mislead political debate and otherwise confuse those who are trying to learn the truth about important public issues. Note that the tricks and traps used are like the flaxen cords in the scripture above—they're pleasing to the worldly mind and that is why they take hold among those who are without God and Christ in their lives.

Latter-day Saints though, are constantly on the lookout for Satan's influence. They recognize his deceitful tactics in tempting our fellow-citizens to disobey God's laws. Let us apply those teachings to the political world so we can avoid the flaxen lies of the adversary and help others break free of them also.

Chapter 8

Separating the Wheat from the Chaff

(Seeing through mainstream media deception)

- Chaff = Bias & Spin
- Liberal Bias in the Mainstream Media
- Anchors, Correspondents and Other Important Deliverers of News
- Sprinkling The Truth With Lies
- Types of Spin:
  - *Personal Attack/Attacking Motives Spin*
  - *Story Selection Spin*
  - *Label Spin*
  - *S[p]ins of Omission*
- Gleaning The Wheat
  - Faster News Cycles and the "New Media"
  - The Internet—Government Sites

- **The Internet—Conservative Organization & "Think Tank" Sites**
- **Talk Radio**
- **Cable/Entertainment Political Television**
- **Columnists**
- **Why this Chapter is Important**

   NOW the Spirit speaketh expressly, that in the latter times some shall...speak lies in hypocrisy; having their conscience seared with a hot iron; 1st Timothy 4:1–2

One reason why many shun politics is because the level of discourse and reporting has sunk so low. The standards for truth telling have deteriorated to the point that reporters and pundits have in many ways become the obstacles, not the enablers, to properly informing ourselves.

A critical part of our political involvement is educating ourselves so that we can make informed choices about what policies to support and whom to vote for. This is not as easy a task as it once was, mostly due to the bias evident in today's mainstream media. It wasn't always like this. Until roughly the 1960's, the media (even though sensationalism had always been with us) pretty much did its basic job, i.e., telling us who, what, when, where and how. Today though, journalism is filled with activists who misuse their job. Instead of objectively reporting news events, they use journalism to slant the facts in an effort to change the world for the better. There's nothing wrong with that desire, but trying to change the world is what our government and we the people are supposed to be doing. The problem lies in how the majority of mainstream journalists define "change for the better."

The mainstream media used to enjoy a monopoly on political reporting and there were few if any other ways to find out the objective truth. In the last 10–15 years or so there has been an explosion in the media and such is no longer the case. There is virtually no reason anymore to watch the major three network television newscasts or read the major newspapers in order to learn about politics and form an opinion. In fact, I recommend against it. In spiritual matters we learn to tune out the voices of the world and the philosophies of men and go directly to the sources of truth. This chapter is about how to tune out political voices of gloom, doom and worldliness and tune into sources of truth. This is of utmost importance—there is only one business mentioned in the Constitution's Bill of

Rights: the press. The reason for that is because it is critical for a moral democracy to have access to truth. The founders wrote the foundations of the freedom of the press/media and left us the people to keep it honest by discerning the truthful grains of wheat and discarding the chaff of untruth, spin, and bias.

Chaff = Bias & Spin

Wheat and chaff are metaphoric scriptural terms that illustrate how the good of the Gospel is allowed to mix with the evil of the world in order for testing and proving to take place before the eventual separation. The political arena works the same way. The chaffy husks of media bias need to be separated from the grains of wheat-truth in order to form a true and faithful political opinion. This exercise has become an enormous undertaking because media bias has made it very difficult to discover the truth. Also, the basic way in which stories are reported has changed over the years so that we are now accustomed to an opinion format as opposed to a fact format. Anyone who remembers pre-1960's reporting knows how it used to be: the reporter was supposed to tell you who, what, where, when and how, and then leave you to draw your own conclusions. Not so anymore.

The stark reality of this hit me while watching the press coverage of the 1996 presidential campaign. (The names and issues are not relevant to the point I'm trying to make so I'll leave them out.)

I was listening to a television political correspondent report on legislation pending in congress. The reporter said that candidate X supported the legislation in question and then quoted the candidate's remarks on the positive effects that would ensue if the legislation passed. Then the reporter quoted candidate Y making several points on why he did not support the legislation and the negative effects that would result from its passing. The reporter then summed up the story with: "I guess we'll have to wait and see in order to know who's right."

I sat there stunned as I thought: "Why didn't the reporter simply read the proposed legislation, report the facts, and then let us make up our own minds?" What passed for reporting was to tell us two people's opinion of the legislation instead of just reporting on what the legislation actually was!

Thus today's news reporting is half the reason why many political issues are so hard to grasp. The other half is a phenomenon of the last 50 years—government has grown so large that the complex policies, laws, rules and statutes are in some cases tremendously difficult to grasp. This combination of large, complex government, coupled with personal bias, makes it much easier for biased journalists to present any issue in virtually any light—positive or negative. It takes effort on our part to discern the truth. This chapter will tackle the major types of media spin and bias.

Liberal Bias in the Mainstream Media

The experience I cited in the previous section is a good example of how journalism standards have deteriorated in recent years. Many news programs and newspapers are little more than gossip sheets, reporting opinions (without letting you know that they're opinions) instead of reporting facts. When facts are mentioned, most of the time they are misapplied or carefully selected in order to slant the story toward a certain side.

Liberal Bias is a much-disputed phenomenon and many studies have been carried out in order to prove it, (such as the abnormally high percentages of journalists who vote to the left of the political spectrum as opposed to the normal statistical percentages reflected in other professions.) But if "truth is knowledge of things as they are" (D&C 93:24), and we're supposed to be seekers of truth, we'd better make sure we're not getting a filtered set of "things as they are." I consider the following instances to be common examples of media bias. I would encourage you to examine each and then spend some time looking for the tactics described as you watch and read the news. Media bias is a very subtle phenomenon, and as the scriptures say, "...the serpent was more subtle than any beast of the field." I don't think anyone in the media is an agent of Satan, but his techniques have been used by the unwitting throughout earth's history. He has deceived many into supporting laws and policy that help to destroy families. Reporting is shaded to make some policies and positions appear more rational, more mainstream, more normal, while trying to make the traditional appear to be radical, extreme, and out-of-touch with mainstream America.

A Word on Complexity

You will note that in most of the media bias instances that you're about to read, I need to preface it with an explanation of the policy surrounding the rules, laws, regulations, statutes, etc. As mentioned previously, this is because our government has grown so huge that all of its programs, laws and statutes are sometimes difficult to comprehend. Unlike the plain and simple truths of the Gospel, much of politics today is very complex, and that's what those who wish to destroy the Constitution are depending on; that you will not be determined enough to fight through the complexity to get at the truth. Unfortunately, we're paying the price for generations of voters who did just that and tuned out when these massive new government programs were introduced and then subsequently expanded. Many did not take the time to read even a few of the thousands of pages of legislation and un-constitutional laws that slipped past "We the people."

Anchors, Correspondents and Other Important Deliverers of News

Though their numbers are declining, most Americans still get their television news from the big three broadcast networks. In times past, the network news was not a risky way to inform oneself of current events, but it is today.

The following is a good example of how the three big network anchors reported on similar actions regarding abortion policy taken by Presidents Bill Clinton and George W. Bush shortly after both took office.

Background: We all know that abortion has been legal since the Roe v. Wade decision in 1973, but the federal government has certain policy powers over funds that are distributed to international organizations that counsel young women on abortion. One of Bill Clinton's first acts as president was to roll back many of the restrictions on abortion funding that had been put in place during the Ronald Reagan and George H.W. Bush presidencies. One of George W. Bush's first acts as president was to put those restrictions back in place.

Here's how the anchors from the big three networks reported on President Clinton:

- "President Clinton keeps his word on abortion rights. President Clinton kept a promise today on the 20th anniversary of the Supreme Court decision legalizing abortion. Mr. Clinton signed presidential memoranda rolling back many of the restrictions imposed by his predecessors."
—Peter Jennings, ABC World News Tonight, January 22nd, 1993

- "Today, President Clinton kept a campaign promise and it came on the 20th anniversary of Roe vs. Wade legalizing abortion."
—Tom Brokaw, NBC Nightly News, January 22nd, 1993

- "On the anniversary of Roe vs. Wade, President Clinton fulfills a promise, supporting abortion rights. It was 20 years ago today, the United States Supreme Court handed down its landmark abortion rights ruling, and the controversy hasn't stopped since. Today, with the stroke of a pen, President Clinton delivered on his campaign promise to cancel several anti-abortion regulations of the Reagan-Bush years."
—Dan Rather, CBS Evening News, January 22nd, 1993

Here's how the coverage went for President George W. Bush in January 2001:

- "One of the president's first actions was designed to appeal to anti-abortion conservatives. The president signed an order reinstating a Reagan-era policy that prohibited federal funding of family planning groups that provided abortion counseling services overseas."—Peter Jennings

- "This was President Bush's first day at the office and he did something to quickly please the right flank in his party: He reinstituted an anti-abortion policy that had been in place during his father's term and the Reagan presidency but was lifted during the Clinton years."—Dan Rather

- "We'll begin with the new president's very active day, which started on a controversial note."—Tom Brokaw

Subtle, aren't they? Note the language; Bill Clinton "keeps his word," "kept a campaign promise," "fulfills a promise, whereas in Bush's case, the anchor's tones are judgmental in the negative. Note that Bush was "appeal[ing] to anti-abortion conservatives," to "quickly please the right flank in his party," and he "started on a controversial note." The three networks all combined their slanted language with another much-used technique—that of labeling anti-abortion proponents as "right-wing," while hardly ever talking about democrats as "left-wing." We should always be on the alert when only one side gets labeled, no matter if it's left or right.

It's also important to notice the almost lock-step similarities in the way the stories are written. ABC, NBC, and CBS are supposedly independent news entities, but the stories read as if the same person wrote them. That's not statistically possible between two sets of three stories, written eight years apart supposedly by three different people at three different and competing networks.

The difference between the reporting on these two events is not very subtle when viewed all together in one place: President Clinton honored his promises, while Bush, on the other hand, only paid attention to the "right flank" of his party. It's important to listen to the language and word choices of those who deliver the news. Facts are very different from labels. Anytime you hear more label language, than fact language, go somewhere else for your news.

Sprinkling The Truth With Lies

> ...*then your eyes shall be opened, and ye shall be as gods, knowing good and evil.* (Genesis 3: 5)

When Satan deceived Adam and Eve in the Garden of Eden, he did so by using information that contained some truth, but was as a whole, not very truthful. Adam and Eve did indeed become as Gods (in a limited way, after eating the fruit they could discern good from evil), but they also became eligible for death. (Religious note: I know this was in God's plan and was supposed to happen, but we're looking at the technique here!) This particular media bias technique involves the very same tactic: relaying what is really dishonest information, sprinkled with some elements of truth.

This occurs most frequently when any person or organization advocates slowing the runaway growth of any large government program. They are immediately accused of "cutting" funds to the _____ (fill in blank: "the poor," "the children," "the elderly," etc.) The "Mediscare" campaign run by democrats in 1995 is a prime example.

Background: To understand this example we need to define what "baseline budgeting" is. Baseline budgeting is a Washington D.C. way of budgeting that automatically assumes next year's budget will be larger by an imaginary number called "the baseline." (This "baseline" figure is arrived at by factoring for population increase along with other "technical" measures that are nebulous at best.) For example, a government program that costs $100 billion one year is automatically figured for the next year using baseline adjustments which means it will take $108 billion the next year in order to continue at the same level of effectiveness.

So it doesn't matter if a program is successful in creating fewer dependents by helping them become independent. It is just automatically assumed that every program budget will increase by large percentages every single year. And here's where the bias comes in:

> ***Anytime anyone proposes a budget number that's below the baseline, even though the total cost of the program still increases, those responsible are accused of "cutting" the program, when in reality, the growth of the program is being slowed, not cut.***

That's what happened with "Mediscare"—in 1995 Republicans tried to slow the runaway growth of this program with a proposal that included a $270 billion reduction in growth, but with spending still increasing by 7% over the previous year. The press uniformly reported that Republicans wanted to cut Medicare.

Here's an amazing analysis by MediaWatch of how the reporting on this story was slanted:

> "MediaWatch analysts reviewed 1,134 news stories in three newspapers (The New York Times, The Washington Post, USA Today) and three news magazines (Newsweek, Time, U.S. News & World Report) from January 1, 1995 to June 30, 1996. Employing the Nexis news data retrieval system to secure every news mention of "Medicare" within 10 words of "cut," "reduce," "slash," "scale back," and "savings," analysts found 1,060 examples of journalists describing Medicare "cuts."

So whenever you hear of politicians or parties wanting to "cut" a government program, read the legislation and find out what the real story is. It's very rare that a government program gets cut. As Ronald Reagan said: "Government programs are the nearest thing to eternal life we'll ever see on earth."

Types of Spin

Much of what the mainstream media reports involves some kind of spin, as opposed to good old-fashioned reporting. (And when I say mainstream media, I'm referring to major network television broadcasts on ABC, NBC, CBS, National Public Radio & Television, and most major newspapers.) Spin is the art of coloring or shading a story so that it appears a certain way instead of simply reporting the facts. There are many types of Spin Bias used by the mainstream media. Here are some examples:

Personal Attack/Attacking Motives Spin

Anytime journalists report comments that may sound like rational arguments, but are really attacks on the person or their motives, you are being spun. The important question to ask oneself is:

"Do the person's comments deal with the substance of the policy, or are they attacks on the other person or their alleged motives?" If the answer is the latter, beware.

Example—Minimum Wage:
Spin
"People who want to keep the minimum wage where it is are just trying to help big business and have no regard for the poor"
No Spin
"Studies actually show that the minimum wage does not cost jobs. The stud-

ies by Krueger and Card show that the minimum wage probably reduces poverty."

Story Selection Spin

This technique is very subtle; it's where the newspaper or news show highlights a pattern of news stories that coincide with the agenda of one side while ignoring stories that agree with the other side's agenda. The most common occurrence of this spin is when a media outlet decides to do a story on a study released by a liberal group, but ignores studies on the same or similar topics released by conservative groups.

> Example—The Eighties
> Newspapers and television stations regularly highlight studies showing how the rich got tax breaks in the '80s while homelessness or other social problems were caused or made worse by "Reagan era budget cuts."
> Many studies by conservative organizations, such as the Heritage Foundation and the Cato Institute, revealed how the rich paid more taxes, social spending was not cut, and social problems were worsened by a breakdown in moral and family values. The American Association of Fund Raising Counsel found that charitable contributions by individuals increased dramatically in the '80s. Those conservative studies were rarely, if ever, reported. But when a liberal group issued studies showing how the rich got richer, the mainstream media trumpeted it loud and long. We live with the results of that spin today. Many believe that the 80's were years of disproportionate greed, while the 90's, a significantly more economically successful decade, was more compassionate because presidents from different parties were in office.

Label Spin

When you read and hear labels attached to conservatives but not to liberals, or when more extreme labels are used for conservatives than for liberals, you'll know you're being subjected to Label Spin.

This ability to frame stories by applying labels to certain politicians, activists and groups is among the media's most subtle and powerful techniques. Remember, though, that labels tell you as much about the person applying the labels as they tell about the person being labeled. A good example is the following excerpt from the 1992 Los Angeles Times in its "Education Election Kit" for teachers. The kit offered the following definitions:

"Conservative: An individual or policy that opposes change in political and social matters."

"Liberal: An individual or policy that favors change in political and social matters. It can also imply tolerance and open-mindedness."

The tag on the liberal definition is about as obvious as spin gets.

President Ezra Taft Benson and other staunch anti-communists were, and are still, referred to as "right-wing," simply for being anti-communist. There is no doubt that President Benson was a conservative, but he certainly did not represent the right wing of the Republican Party.

Be on the lookout for the following labels that are applied to mainstream constitutional conservatives: "far right," "ultra-conservative," or "right-wing extremists." By the same token, be on the lookout for false labels on the left side of the political aisle. There are those in this country who advocate radical ideas such as the overthrow of the Constitution or the abolition of private property, but they are not identified by any term that would let the news consumer know they held such beliefs. Instead they are given labels such as: "progressives," "liberals," or "moderates." The media regularly and rightfully labels conservative groups as conservative, while liberal groups are described in neutral terms such as "women's group" or "civil rights group," or even favorable terms such as "children's rights supporters," or "free-speech activists."

During election campaigns is when the liberal media practices lots of Label Spin. When conservatives talk about their positions, the media call it "appealing to the far right of the party," in an effort to make those who agree feel that they're not part of the mainstream. When liberals outline their positions, the press will almost always frame them as appealing to normal rational people.

Another type of Label Spin occurs when a reporter not only fails to identify a liberal as a liberal, but instead uses a label, such as "an expert" or "independent consumer group," thus lending an air of unmerited authority to a source. Labels aren't necessarily bad in and of themselves. With all the different parties, organizations, politicians and programs out there, some labels must exist so we can sift and classify information and not have to study every issue from scratch in order to reach the correct position. So not all labeling is biased or wrong. We need to be able to recognize incorrect labels though so we can tell when we're getting news that is ideologically slanted. A story calling Senator Hatch "conservative" is accurate, as would be a reporter's reference to Rush Limbaugh as "the conservative radio talk show host." However, your "media bias" antenna should be on full alert if you hear a story that labels conservatives as such but then does not label liberal sources as liberal. A balanced promo would go something like: "Rush Limbaugh will be the conservative counterpart on tonight's show, across the table from the liberal Lanny Davis." The spin promo would be: "Rush Limbaugh will be the conservative counterpart on tonight's show, across the table from ex-presidential adviser, Lanny Davis."

S[p]ins of Omission

Omission Spin is where the media leaves out facts that tend to disprove one side or the other's claims or positions.

This is a bit tougher to ferret out, as this kind of bias requires that one be well informed about the issue in question. Once you do though, you'll know the various perspectives on the important issues and you'll recognize when one side is left out. Omission spin usually occurs either:

A. Within one story, or

B. Over the long term as a particular media entity reports one set of facts or events, but not another.

Omission spin over the long term is also very evident in the way the tax issue is reported. The media will quote any liberal politician who claims "the rich need to be paying their fair share." The facts are never ever mentioned by the mainstream media, which are well illustrated by the following table:

Percentiles Ranked by AGI*	Adjusted Gross Income	% of Total Income Tax Paid
Top 1%	$292,913	33.89%
Top 5%	$127,904	53.25%
Top 10%	$92,754	64.89%
Top 25%	$56,085	82.90%
Top 50%	$28,528	96.03%
Bottom 50%	<$28,528	3.97%

*AGI=Adjusted gross Income
Source: Internal Revenue Service for 2001 Tax Year

A few things jump right out when examining this table. Especially the notable "big picture" omissions by the media when they show politicians talk about going after the rich to pay a greater share of taxes:

1. What is the definition of rich?

2. What is the definition of someone's "fair share?"

Any way you slice it; the rich are paying their fair share and then some. (I don't know about you, but I don't consider those who make over $127,000 dollars a year "rich", yet these top 5% are paying 50% of the total tax burden.) Do you also notice how mainstream interviewers ***never*** ask these politicians to define rich or what constitutes someone's fair share?

The way education funding is reported is another good example of Omission Spin within a single news story. Many follow this type of pattern: The media reports the need for increased spending on education, (which is an opinion—not a news story.)

1. The story will focus on the need to improve test scores and more taxpayer funding is invariably the solution.
2. 99% of the time the reporter will not explore any other possible causes for the low scores.
3. The story will leave out any mention of the many school systems, (not only in the U.S., but around the world), that spend less and achieve higher student test scores.

Education funding news stories tend to focus on sympathy generating and emotional aspects of the issue. Of course children should be a top priority, and it is certain that they are our future; there is no one that will disagree on those points. That is not at issue though; the news is doing a disservice by reporting misdirection that leaves out other possible causes behind the problem. This is to lead you away from the main reasons for the low test scores—the ever-increasing cadre of administrators, bureaucrats and teacher's unions.

As news consumers, we should also be concerned about what we're ***not*** seeing. The media leave whole areas uncovered and that's a huge impediment to Latter-day Saints becoming truly educated and informed on the issues.

Gleaning The Wheat

With all that media chaff out there, you might be asking yourself: "How is a Latter-day Saint supposed to glean the kernels of truth about important news events instead of believing the spin?" There are ways, but just as with any search for truth, it takes some time, effort and thought.

Faster News Cycles and the "New Media"

The new media have begun to overshadow the old media of newspapers and broadcast television in today's political process. Nontraditional media such as talk radio, the Internet and cable/entertainment TV political shows are very useful in our quest for truth for a very important reason. News cycles are speeding along faster and faster every year. From the 1600's until the late 1940's news events took a long time to develop and then to affect people's lives, simply because it took such a long time for a newspaper to obtain the news and then get it into people's hands. The advent of television greatly sped up that process. In today's world, news cycles have sped up to the point where public figures know that their public image is being affected at almost every moment of the day.

In the past, politicians knew that they could enact legislation and that it would take some time for the new law to have an effect before people would really know enough about it to start giving feedback. Not so anymore. Now, the news process:

A. Enables people to get information about politician's record (instead of what they **say** about their record)

B. Is like a gossip chain that sometimes creates more talk about the sensational than the substantive, thus obscuring facts.

The Internet—Government Sites

The Internet is very useful for getting the facts, but one has to know where the sources of the good information are because there's plenty of bad information out there too. When it comes to politics, learn to use your federal, state and local government's web sites. I spend a fair amount of time on the federal government's web site. There are many, but the best place to start is the U.S. Congress' web site at: Thomas.loc.gov. That site also has links to the judicial and executive branches of the federal government. Bottom Line: Don't just believe what the media says the government is doing, go and look at what they're actually doing! Most of what our government does, by law, must be published. Reading even a portion of the mountains of information will also carry the benefit of transforming most anyone into a small government conservative, because once you start wandering around just a few of the millions of web pages containing the millions upon millions of pieces of information about what our government is involved in, you will realize that there are all sorts of opportunities for abuse and no possible way to keep track of it all. Obviously I can't list them all here, but all 50 states and counties and cities have web sites too. The most important thing to learn is how to use a search engine so you can find the important sites you're looking for with the correct, and in-context information.

The Internet—Conservative Organization & "Think Tank" Sites

There are many conservative organizations and think tanks out there and their websites can inform you regarding facts, and voting records. See the appendix for a good selection.

Talk Radio

Talk radio is one of the most effective public forums because it's more honest that traditional mainstream media. Most of talk radio is conservative because that is where conservatives were forced to turn when the mainstream television and newspapers became so biased in espousing the liberal point of view in its coverage. There are some liberal radio talk show hosts, but none that even approach the success of conservatives. Some might say that talk radio is just as biased to the conservative viewpoint, but that reasoning misses a supremely important point:

> *Conservative talk radio states that it is conservative, thus it is an honest medium, and anyone who listens can decide for themselves whether or not they agree, whereas the mainstream media does not admit its bias, thus concealing its editorial viewpoint and passing it off as news.*

Talk radio is a way to find out about all those things the mainstream will not tell you; like baseline budgeting, who really pays most of the taxes, etc. I know because that's where I started learning about the things the mainstream media had been omitting from my nightly news and morning paper! Another important difference is that talk radio allows for phone calls from people who are not politicians and media employees thus enabling one to get an idea of what other fellow-citizens from all sides are thinking. That's something you will not get with mainstream television and newspapers that eliminate conservative views and opinions. The points of view coming from the mainstream journalist elite have very little in common with what the average American experiences in his daily life.

Cable/Entertainment Political Television

These shows are pretty much the talk radio of the television airwaves. Anyone with a cable television subscription knows about these shows because they pretty much all share the same format: The host or hosts (usually one representing the "conservative" and another, the "liberal" side of the political spectrum), discuss the major issues of the day and include guests or panels of guests in an effort to present both sides of an issue. Unfortunately many of the guests tend to be argumentative and spend a lot of time spinning, interrupting or trying to out shout the host or other guest(s). However, that can be very instructive in and of itself, because you will be able witness and get a feel for the kinds of people who are backing the various candidates and causes. You can also see who's reporting spin as fact, and who is using facts to frame the issue.

Columnists

I can't over-emphasize what a great way regular reading of columnists is to learn about politics. Good columnists write about current political issues, combined with reasoned opinion; even though they have their own point of view, be it liberal or conservative, you can get a good summary of a given issue in a very short amount of time. If you balance the columnists you read between liberal, independent, and conservative, you immunize yourself from spin because you've heard each side's facts and spin in a short amount of time. You can then check the facts, see whose espousing the correct position, and come to the right conclusion about which side to support.

Reading columnists is also a much more entertaining way to inform yourself on the issues because one of the biggest requirements for becoming a successful, widely-read columnist is to be entertaining while also being informative and thought provoking. As with everything, it's a good idea to be balanced by reading columnists on all sides. You'll immediately be in touch with most perspectives on the major issues because conservative columnists use those facts and rationale that support the limited constitutional government point of view, while liberal columnists utilize those which advance the government growth, progressive stance, etc. I've included a good starter list of columnists of all stripes in the appendix of this book. I urge you to choose a selection of those that appeal to you most, find the websites, (or subscribe to the publications), that run their columns and start reading them on a regular basis as part of one's own continuing political education.
Columnist Caveat: Reading Columnists is Like Learning to Read the Scriptures—It's Tough in the Early Going!

Many find it difficult in the beginning to get value out of reading columnists and you might find yourself in that group. Keep with it. Reading columnists is in some ways comparable to reading the scriptures because politics has its own language that takes some getting used to. The terms most columnists sprinkle their columns with are different mostly because our government and its multitude of programs have grown so huge that it's impossible to talk about them in normal every-day terms. So if you start reading some of these people and you have a hard time following them, *just keep reading*—pretty soon the 'ye' 'thee', and 'verily' language of politics will begin to make sense to you.

Why this Chapter is Important

And that wicked one cometh and taketh away light and truth…(D&C 93:39)

The principles in this chapter are a necessity in order to recognize the opposition's attacks on the Constitution because the wicked one does not come out and openly state his goal. His representatives disguise themselves in sheep's clothing of truth, but inwardly they are truly ravening wolves. Once we are able to discern these political tactics and techniques, we can eliminate them quickly, and then build strong channels of political truth into our everyday lives. Just as in spiritually choosing the right we need the guidance of truth as manifested by the Holy Ghost, we can't make the right political votes and choices if our conclusions are based on faulty or incomplete information, spin or political gossip.

Chapter 9

Discussing Politics, Religion (and other touchy subjects)

- **Similarities Between Religion and Politics**
- **Winning Hearts and Minds**
- **Avoid Statistics "Bashing"**
- **Other Things to Avoid**
- **Be Involved**
- **Find Commonality**
- **Agree to Disagree**

Similarities Between Religion and Politics

One of the best ways to improve one's understanding of politics (as with anything else) is by discussing it with knowledgeable people on both sides of the issues. Politics, just like religion, is a sensitive subject though, and that is why many say "you can't discuss religion and politics!" As Latter-day Saints we have been commanded to share the Gospel with others; if we work at that, the same obstacles we overcome in talking about our religion will help us in discussing politics with our friends, neighbors and associates.

Religion and politics deal with some of the most important questions of human existence:

Religion

- Where do we come from?
- Why are we here on earth?
- What happens after this life ends?

Politics

- What is the best way to govern ourselves as a society?
- How do we decide who receives (and shares) power and authority?
- Over what aspects of our families, lives and property should the government exercise power?

Religion and politics are similar because both involve a set of beliefs based on faith and feelings as opposed to facts and statistics. I realize that might not quite seem true at first blush, but consider this question:

How many people have changed religions because of scripture bashing and how many people have changed their political affiliation because of statistics?

The answer is very few. Politics and religion have much more in common than is generally thought. That makes active Latter-day Saints some of the best-equipped people to discuss politics.

When discussing politics it's important to avoid pointless arguments that lead to contention and bad feelings. Even among church members I have found that we do not all think alike on the issues even though we all think we are in line with the position a Latter-day Saint should hold. That's why it's all the more important to discuss politics amongst ourselves and build political consensus based on our religious principles. Brigham Young said:

> *"Joseph used to say, "When you get the Latter-day Saints to agree on any point, you may know it is the voice of God."*
> Discourses of Brigham Young, 12:301, p.469

No matter whether we are discussing politics with those who share, or do not share our view, there are a number of useful things to remember.

Winning Hearts and Minds

There is an expression: "winning hearts and minds," and I believe it describes perfectly the process of political persuasion…it is the political equivalent of conversion. It is the process someone goes through as they take an honest look at themselves and what they believe and consider changing their beliefs. The goal of "winning of hearts and minds" is an absolutely vital attitude to have when discussing politics. If we are not focused on that goal then we are just concerned with being right, and being right is not nearly so satisfying as bringing someone to knowledge of the truth. A good example of this process is the abolitionist movement of the first four score and seven years of this country's history.

Slavery in the United States is a legacy we wish had not happened. There is a simple reason why the slaves were not freed when this country was formed. If the framers of the Constitution had insisted upon emancipation of the slaves, the southern states would not have ratified the Constitution and the country would have continued its disintegration under the Articles of Confederation and the nation we enjoy today would not exist. That did not faze the abolition movement though—they merely set about winning the hearts and minds of the nation. From 1776 to the 1830's they existed only as fragmented religious groups that opposed the practice of slavery. Then in 1831 the American Anti-Slavery Society was formed with other similar organizations to follow. In 1842 these groups formed a lobbying arm to work on congress and in 1856 threw their support to the new Republican party. And the rest, as they say, is history.

The important point for us here is learning the process of winning hearts and minds. Let's go back to the issue used previously—abortion. The practice of abortion makes me both cringe and cry as I contemplate the millions of souls whose lives have been taken by this practice. If we liken ourselves to the abolitionists, we are in the early to middle phase where we exist both as a number of separate religious groups and lobbying organizations. We will need to agree to disagree with those who think otherwise and exercise patient moral suasion as our principal practice. Recognizing people's right to disagree and showing that we are committed to their freedom is the first step in convincing them of the truth.

Avoid Statistics "Bashing"

When discussing one's political position with someone who holds the opposite view, citing facts and statistics alone usually has the same effect as trying to convert someone simply by citing biblical references. It will either…
A) alienate those who are not familiar with the statistics and figures, or

B) cause a "Bible Bashing"-type argument to ensue,

...either way, it will *not* produce converts.

Facts, just like scriptures, should be used in a supporting role. People respond politically in their hearts just as much or many times more than they do with their heads. Those who have successful political and religious conversations shy away from dependence on sheer factual evidence to win people over.

Other Things to Avoid

There are a number of other debate and discussion habits that tend to shut down people's hearts and minds before they have a chance to hear what we have to say. Before telling what they are I'd like to share a personal experience.

I belong to a number of online political chat groups; in one particular forum there's a gentleman whom I'll call Greg, with whom I disagreed vehemently on almost every issue. We used to trade facts and barbs, and when that produced no change in the other, insulting comments. I'm not proud to make that admission. I wish I had behaved differently. There was tension between us that affected the whole group and cast a cloud over the interchanges. I'm glad to report though that it did not end that way. One day I thought to myself: "I hate this. I may disagree vehemently with Greg on many issues, but for one thing, he is one of the most intelligent people I've ever debated. Also, he is a law-abiding, tax-paying citizen of this country. That means in the big picture he is part of the solution, not part of the problem; I'd rather convert him than condemn him."

Things changed for the better since that day. I approached discussions differently; Greg felt that change and responded in kind. We still disagree vehemently on the same issues, except now there is no acrimony. We share mutual respect instead of disdain. I found that there are certain ways of framing issues and positions that lead to the honest interchange of ideas. Here are some things to avoid…

Name Calling—When we begin a discussion with something like: "President X is such a liar, how can we ever believe what he says about Social Security reform? The person you're talking with may like President X a lot, and if that's the case, you'll never get to the next subtopic on Social Security. That person will be ignoring everything you say from that point on. President X may well be a liar, but name-calling to that effect will not advance the discussion. Better to restate your support for taking care of the elderly and then bring up how to better reform Social Security.

Stating opinion as fact—"Senator X's plan for welfare reform is racist and discriminates against the poor." Again, Senator X's plan may indeed discriminate against certain segments of society, but if your discussion partner has a parent or spouse that favors the plan, then the talking may continue, but the discussion is over. A better way to approach it is to cite the part of the plan you're talking about and then ask if that seems discriminatory.

Mind Reading—This is a technique used by some to demonstrate how they know someone's feelings or hidden agenda. Once in my chat group, someone who supported the war in Afghanistan and Iraq asked one of those who opposed the war if they at least supported liberating those countries even if it was just because of how those countries mistreated women. The person responded: "I think they just want to go on about business as usual blowing up developing countries. George W. Bush doesn't care one whit about women in Afghanistan." Whenever we presume to be inside someone's head and to know their thoughts and emotions, we're going to have a negative effect on our efforts to win hearts and minds.

Misdirection—This tactic is used when somebody makes a point about someone or something and is answered with something negative about a completely different aspect in order to draw attention away from the first point. A good example from my chat group:
Me: "It put American lives in danger when Senator X leaked military secrets and had to resign as vice chairman of the senate intelligence committee."
Jan (not her real name): "Maybe he values democracy over deceit and hypocrisy, instead of being secretive like our current president."
You'll note how the person failed to respond to the point that was being made and tried to direct attention away from the leak to someone else's behavior." (Note: This is a favorite tactic of politicians when being interviewed.)

Using the extreme fringe—This is where someone uses the fanatics on either side of a given issue in order to demonize the mainstream. A good example is the abortion issue. The pro-abortion side regularly characterizes and lumps those that are anti-abortion in with the people who murder abortion doctors. This is unfair and turns off people that are trying to come to an understanding of the issues. Nobody wants to think of him or herself as sharing the same beliefs as people who are hateful or who commit crimes or are otherwise unfavorably viewed by the majority.

Political beliefs are similar to religious beliefs in many ways. Many times political positions and heroes are taught and handed down by family and authority figures. Because those relatives and friends are respected by those we are speaking to, it will take more than facts or intellectual bullying to bring people around to our side of the issue. We must become the kinds of people that merit trust and friendship when we're discussing politics. That way the positions we espouse will carry equal sway with those that have been taught by relatives and friends without unintentionally insulting those trusted figures.

Be Involved

People usually respect the opinions of people who care enough to get involved in some form or another. Everyone has an opinion, but those who read; vote; write letters to the editor of the local paper, and serve in volunteer, charitable, or school functions are those whose opinions carry weight. This principle of persuasion works in the political the same way as a testimony does in the spiritual; it's one thing to say one has a strong belief, but if that person spends no time doing what God has asked, the testimony carries less persuasive influence. Those who involve themselves in civic and political issues and do more than just express their opinions have greater power to win hearts and minds.

I realize that's no easy chore. It's difficult to add more items to a growing list of family and church activities. Just like anything else, start small and start with the parts that matter most to you. Here's a short list of things anyone can do to become more involved, and that also don't require a major investment of time and effort. (The next chapter will discuss our personal involvement in more detail.)

- Start Local—Some of the easiest political issues to become familiar with, and passionate about, are local. Find out what your school board and your city council are doing. Chances are someone close to you is a teacher or local government employee and can help you familiarize yourself with the issues. If not, attend a city council or school board meeting and you will most likely hear something that you will feel passionate about.
- Put Up Yard Signs—Once you take a position on a candidate or ballot initiative, get one of their yard signs or bumper stickers and display it in the weeks preceding an election. Candidates and causes are anxious to give them out; what's more, it's a very clear statement to your friends and

neighbors that you have enough courage for an outward display of your convictions.

- Read columnists and pundits for 15 minutes a day—News articles are already biased these days, so you might as well read those who will admit they have a conservative or liberal viewpoint. Reading these opinion pieces will not make you a mind-numbed robot. They will help you consolidate and formulate your own views as you will become able to follow the thinking and decide for yourself. (See the appendix for a columnist 'starter' list of recommendations.)

Find Commonality

It doesn't matter whether it's over politics or religion, one of Satan's principal techniques in accomplishing his ends is for men and women to fight and quarrel with one another. If he can get people to generate ill feelings among themselves, it doesn't matter who's right and who's wrong—Lucifer has won. In his October 1974 General Conference talk, Elder Theodore M. Burton said:

> "God, who knows all things from the beginning, knew that in the last days Satan would exert every effort to destroy the work of God…He will try to influence men as never before to destroy one another by ***dissension***, opposition, selfishness, wars, riots, and destructions. If he can get people to ***quarrel*** with one another, *they will inevitably destroy themselves.*"
> Ensign, Nov. 1974, 54 (italics & bold, author's)

Once while traveling by air, I was sitting in my seat reading the Book of Mormon, waiting for the flight to depart when the passenger seated next to me looked at what I was reading and introduced himself. It turned out that he was a Methodist minister and was familiar with the Book of Mormon, at which point he asked me one of those "confrontational" questions about the truthfulness of Joseph Smith and the Book of Mormon. When he did, I got that "oh no, here we go" feeling we get when someone brings up polygamy, or the Word of Wisdom. The Spirit directed me to another way of answering his query. I replied that I would answer his question, but first I wanted to find out what he believed about religion in general so I could give him my answer in such a way as to be satisfying to him.

He agreed and so I said:

> "We believe that Jesus Christ is the only begotten Son of God, who took upon him our sins so that we might have an opportunity to return to God's presence. Do you believe that in your church?"

The minister indicated that he did, so I continued:

> "We believe that men are responsible for their actions and that through baptism by immersion, we show God that we are willing to follow his Son and do his will. Is that your church's belief too?"

He again indicated that he agreed.

I asked a few other similar questions, which then led us into a discussion that touched on church, family, friends and even world politics and the spiritual ramifications of current events. Eventually I answered his initial question, but the answer didn't lead to another confrontational question. I bore my testimony and by the time the flight ended we parted as two people who, though they disagreed, had shared a pleasant and meaningful time discussing things that are important to them, instead of two people who had just had a fruitless tug-of-war.

Why *commonality is important*—This may be a story about discussing religion, but the same principle operates when discussing politics. The biggest wedge to understanding is the perception that people are at complete opposites. I am convinced that both Satan and the mainstream press derive great benefit from having Americans believe that conservatives and liberals are at different ends of the political spectrum. (Notice that the press will tend to focus on issues like abortion and other controversial themes in order to enforce that perception.) I believe that most U.S. citizens share many common views about such things as personal responsibility and accountability for one's actions, education, national defense and other bedrocks of our political foundation. When we focus on commonality first, others tend to be receptive to listening and discussing areas of disagreement with a more open frame of mind.

Agree to Disagree

No matter how much you find in common with others, if you have enough political discussions, you will have to discuss the big issues on which we Latter-day Saints differ with many. In those cases it's important to realize that most of the time you will never persuade someone on the basis of one conversation and you will need to make an even greater effort to prevent argument and dissension. One of the best ways to do that is to simply recognize the validity of the other person's viewpoint. That is not to say that you agree with the person, but it does keep the dialogue going (and ending up) in a civil fashion. Many times I have said something along the lines of: "I realize that we disagree on the major points of the abortion issue, but maybe we could discuss partial-birth abortion and its effects."

Agreeing to disagree is integral to the process of "winning of hearts and minds" process. Recognizing that someone has arrived at their point of view through thoughtful consideration lets that person know that we care about more than just being right or winning a debate. Once we develop these attitudes that make discussing religion and politics less stressful and confrontational, we will look forward to the opportunity to do so. We will develop friendships and associations with others that will allow them to get to know us, and instead of gaining a reputation of having bitter arguments; we will be known as people who win spirits, hearts and minds by caring and gentle persuasion.

CHAPTER 10

Get Involved—Local, State, Federal...Pick One

- Apathy
- Making it a personal commitment
- **Start with something close to you**
- **Federal, State, Local...**
- **Ramping up**
- **Do what you do best...**

Apathy

Elder Neal A. Maxwell (who earned his bachelor's and master's degrees in political science from the University of Utah), said:

> "It was G. K. Chesterton who first warned us about what can happen to a "tired democracy," a democracy in which the people are willing to leave their chores to a few "lonely sentinels." There are many who now believe that American democracy is, in fact, a "tired democracy," with "deliberate apathy" eating away at the vitals of our society."

Neal A. Maxwell, "The Lonely Sentinels of Democracy," New Era, July 1972, p.47

Symptoms of this kind of tiredness are much in evidence in our country today. There are times when one observes the world of politics and says: "I don't see how voters can stand for something this outrageous!" The reason outrageous things are gotten away with can generally be answered in a single word: apathy. Let's take a political and religious issue that's not going to be politically resolved any time soon: same-sex "marriage." Polls indicate that a large majority of American voters oppose same-sex marriage, yet our elected representatives do not receive a lot of voter input regarding the attack on this important institution. What's the cause? Apathy and the fear of men. Some simply do not want to rouse themselves, others do not want to appear to be too judgmental in today's "tolerant" environment.

To many, marriage is not a critical issue, but not to Latter-day Saints. This is a prime political arena for us to roll up our sleeves and get to work. This issue has the potential to ultimately destroy the institution of marriage, and as goes marriage, so goes the family. Apathy is not a problem unique to Latter-day saints. There are Jews and Christians who recognize the vital importance of the family, and thus oppose same-sex "marriage" but are still not speaking up. For many people I think the problem is a lack of faith.

That may sound harsh, but I can't think of any better way to put it. Many seem to have succumbed to a "What's the use?" type of attitude. They believe that the cultural climate has turned so much against us that we'll never be able to stop the advance of societal decay. That kind of apathy dooms us to a world where evil makes the decisions because good lacks the faith to act. Edmund Burke summed it up well:

"The only thing necessary for the triumph of evil is for good men to do nothing."

Making it a personal commitment

> "...the world needs practical religion—it needs applied Christianity . It needs not only to pray, 'Thy kingdom come. Thy will be done in earth, as it is in heaven,' (Matt. 6:10) but also to work for the establishment of divine government among human beings."
> David O. McKay, *Gospel Ideals*, p.294

Getting involved in politics is in many ways like increasing one's level of dedication to the Lord, or magnifying one's calling—for some it is a matter of making time in a busy life, while for others it is a daunting task that seems beyond their capabilities. The common denominator in our world of both religion and politics though is that there are some who see the importance and get involved, and others who participate in the benefits while making no personal sacrifice. At times it may be intimidating because those who believe in the constitutional foundations of this country are no longer in the majority.

A good example of how an active minority has the power to change the course of events can be seen in our own country's independence. In 1760 as revolutionary sentiment began to grow in America, the population of the thirteen colonies was approximately 1,600,000, (about one fourth of whom were slaves.) The best estimates as to how the loyalties of the people were divided are that one-third favored continuing under British colony status; one third favored revolution, and one third was undecided or didn't care. That means that approximately half a million people got involved and created this nation. That minority of 33% worked against or amidst over a million others and accomplished the work of creating the greatest and longest-enduring democracy this world has ever seen. There will always be those who oppose righteousness and there will always be those who do nothing to engage for either side. Thus we see that change is almost always accomplished by minorities…for good or for evil. This is a good thought to keep present if we ever feel too small or that there are not enough of us to accomplish the task we've been charged with.

Start with something close to you

So—How to start then? Politics is a big, expansive field of endeavor and the important thing to remember is that we don't have to swallow this elephant in one gulp. A good way to start is to focus on an area that personally affects or interests us most and then focus on that aspect. As we search out others who feel the same we will find those who share our views; this will add to our resolve and we will become part of the process, line upon line, precept upon precept. Your involvement will be an outward confirmation that you are part of the 33% that is anxiously engaged in working toward the solution instead of those who are doing little or nothing, yet are still participating in the benefits of a democratic republic.

My own personal experience is a fair example of how political involvement can take hold and grow. When I started taking notice of politics in my twenties I realized I had not been taught a lot concerning civics and politics, (the decline of these subjects is a theme for a whole different chapter!) As I started working I looked at all the funds withheld from my paycheck and I wondered what all that money paid for. I started reading economics, and then philosophy, which then instinctively led me toward conservatism. Even though I had been raised by democrats, and considered myself one, I made the same change Ronald Reagan did in the early 1960's. I recognized that the democrat party's elevation of abortion and the welfare state to its principle platform planks had removed it from its Rooseveltian-Truman moorings and was turning it into a party I could not belong to anymore.

After I was married and had a child in the school system, a situation arose in our school district where rapid growth had not been accompanied by the building of new high schools. This made for massive, impersonal high schools with nearly 5,000 students attending them. Most parents did not endorse this approach but had not gathered politically to oppose those who favored these huge schools. The big-school proponents turned out to be a small minority of parents and teachers who wanted the large school 5A rating so the sports teams had a larger talent pool to draw from, while some teachers and bureaucrats derived financial and grant considerations. My wife and I got involved in defeating a bond that would have built no new schools and helped get a subsequent bond that actually addressed the problem. I ran for school board twice after that, but did not win. It was disappointing, but the experience was invaluable.

My point for this chapter is that if you are currently not involved in politics, but would like to start—begin by choosing an issue that is close to what you are experiencing with your family, or are familiar with from work, or in your community. This way you will start from a position of familiarity with the problem and a personal stake in the outcome. Learn about the politics surrounding it; and in today's era of big government, chances are, it will take you a while to educate yourself. Then you will discover that the educational process never ends, because now you are part of the solution, instead of someone who passively reads these things in the paper or sees them on the news. You will be someone whose educated vote is integral to our democracy…and others will seek out your informed opinion.

Federal, State, Local…

Looking around for the elements of the political spectrum that interest you most is an important part of getting involved. Some of the issues that will motivate and drive you may be found at all three levels of government. Education and other similar street sign, property tax and zoning law issues will be found at the municipal, district or county level of government. Each is just as important as the other. The only dynamic that changes is how many people and organizations are involved as the issue gains attention at the national level. The following are just some suggestions to get started.

Federal

If you'd like to get involved in influencing issues at the national level and prefer to spend more time writing letters, emails, and feel more comfortable in very large organizations, then you might enjoy getting involved in presidential politics and in getting good national legislation passed. Obviously this level of involvement means that you join organizations that are necessarily large because you're helping influence voters across the country to support constitutional government.

Involvement at the federal level is generally done by getting active in your party's national efforts as well as nation-wide organizations like the League of Women Voters, the NRA, the Eagle Forum, the American Conservative Union or a number of others.

State

Involvement at the state level can take a number of forms:

- Campaigning for, and lobbying representatives to the U.S. congress
- Campaigning for state officials such as Governor, representatives to the state legislature
- Lobbying the legislature to pass good legislation
- Campaigning for all statewide elections

Participating at the state level means joining groups that work within the state confines. As many states vary in their issues, find something that affects your area directly and then discover who and what groups are working within your state's constitutional bounds for good government. Just as our national charter dictates that the states and not the federal government should handle issues not enumerated in the Constitution; there are issues that should not be handled at the state, but at local county and municipal levels. Working toward good government many times means getting the decision made at the proper level of government.

Local

County, city and local school board education issues are easier for some to start with because many of us have friends and acquaintances who are involved or have read in the local paper just who is doing what. There are certainly groups and organizations one can join, but we can also form a "group of one" by talking to and emailing our friends about initiatives we care about. It doesn't take very many votes to swing local elections and we can really get a good feeling of participation by working towards causes that are close to home.

Ramping up

You're busy and you have a lot to do. Adding political chores to your list of to-dos is perhaps not an attractive proposition. Starting small and ramping up is the key to sustained civic involvement. Here are a number of things that do not take a great deal of time that one can do to get involved; you'll note that they fall into two general categories: informing yourself, or being an influence:

- Ensure that you are registered to vote. Your County Clerk is the place to start.
- Obtain the address, phone numbers, and email addresses for your local, state and federal representatives and when you see something taking place in government that you approve or disapprove of, write a note to the appropriate representative in support or opposition.
- Sign a petition.
- Put up a yard sign for a candidate you endorse
- Email, or talk to your friends and neighbors about a local issue that affects both of you.
- Once a day, read about an issue that interests you in the newspaper or on the Internet. Go to government sources to examine the laws in place and to verify the accuracy of the facts before determining your position.
- Attend a school board or city council meeting.
- Volunteer to do phone or envelope-licking work for a candidate you endorse.
- Write a letter to the editor of your local paper. Keep it short. State your position without attacking the opposing party. Put your emotion into stating the benefits of your position.
- Read the Constitution and The Federalist Papers.
- Read a biography of one of the founding fathers.

- Work at your local voting precinct on election days. It's a wonderful way to make a little money on the side, and you will come to know other involved citizens.
- Run for town council, school board…or something even smaller like precinct chairman.
- If you are not currently able to use a computer, do email, or use the Internet, learn to do so. Electronic means are fast becoming the best political instruments for both educating, communicating, and persuading.

Do what you do best…

No one need do all the things mentioned in the above list. Everyone has different talents and abilities and it behooves us to consider our own when we're looking at increasing our involvement in civic affairs. Not all of us are eloquent speakers, but we all have some degree of writing talent that will grow as we use it. Some of us have the ability to recognize political trends and good candidates and support them. Others of us are well organized and can do much good in establishing campaigns around honorable politicians, causes and initiatives. Some of us are good at being friendly and talking to those around us to make the case for what we believe. Do some soul searching and work at those things to which your abilities are best suited. There is no end to the good we can do if we simply take a look around us and let our principles guide our personal talents in working for the good of our religion, freedom, and government. Each of us has a personal God-given Title of Liberty. One of my greatest hopes in writing this book is that those who read it will be inspired to develop their own passion for politics and wave their personal title of liberty with conviction.

CHAPTER 11
▼

CAST AN INFORMED VOTE (IN <u>EVERY</u> ELECTION!)

- **<u>Every</u> election**
- **Avoid being a one-issue voter**
- **Voting as an individual**
- **Voting with the mind as well as the heart**
- **Have the Brethren spoken?**
- **Voting As One**

There's a popular scripture on instruction and education in the Doctrine and Covenants that begins, *"Teach ye diligently…"* (D&C 88:78). The Lord then lists important things that Latter-day Saints should be diligently teaching and learning, such as, doctrine, the law of the Gospel, and things that pertain to the kingdom of God. The list does not end there though…in verse 79 the Lord cites some other important subjects about which we need to be educating ourselves:

- Things that are at home
- Things which are abroad
- The wars and the perplexities of the nations
- The judgments which are on the land

- Knowledge also of countries and of kingdoms

This type of knowledge is vital for the Latter-day Saint determined to fulfill the charge to befriend and preserve the Constitution by making wise choices at the ballot box.

Every election

Elder Rulon S. Wells stated the following from the tabernacle pulpit:

> *"What a wonderful privilege it is to be a citizen of a republic where every citizen has an equal right. He should then exercise the same for the welfare and exaltation of the people... When we read in our newspaper files of the gross transgression of law all over the land, the people violating the provisions of the Constitution, which we believe has been inspired of God, how our hearts must be filled with indignation against this wanton violation of law. When we...wink at such violations, how humiliated we must feel when we realize that these are the men whom we have chosen to execute the laws, and we are therefore ourselves to blame.* **Indifference to politics, neglect to attend primaries, apathy in matters of such vital importance as the government for which we are directly responsible, will not exonerate us from this blame.***"*

Rulon S. Wells, Conference Report, October 1921, p.81 (bold, author's)

One of our first civic responsibilities is to keep informed as to the various elections in which we are eligible to participate, and then cast a vote. Here are 95% of them:

- General Elections—Held every two years on the first Tuesday in November, (in even numbered years), to elect congressional representatives. Every other general election, (or every four years), includes the presidential ballot.
- Primary Elections—Held every two years, (in even numbered years), to elect each party's candidates for the General Election. The date of the lection depends on when your state parties hold their primary elections.
- County Elections—Are usually combined with a general election, but can be held on other dates to elect Board of Supervisors, County Assessor and a number of other offices, (depending on your county.)

- Municipal Elections—Are usually combined with a general election, but can be held on other dates to elect Mayor, town council, vote on bond issues etc.

- Bond/Ballot Initiative Referendums—State or local bond referendums are sometimes combined with a general election, but can be held on other dates to pass bond and issue-oriented ballot measures. (Ballot initiatives/measures are not held in every state.)

- School Board Elections—Held in accordance with state and/or local school district policy; dates vary.

There are other elections, such as runoffs, additional primaries, etc. This is just to get an idea of the elections in which most of your votes will be cast. In order to find out dates and voting precincts you should contact your state secretary of state, county and city clerks, as well as school districts.

We Americans have a wealth of power and control over our destinies because we live in the freest, most democratic nation ever to exist on the Earth. However, someone once said that a country gets the government it deserves and I agree wholeheartedly with that sentiment. Many times people comment on government problems, as if the blame rests entirely elsewhere, when they themselves, along with many others, failed to get out and vote for government that might have behaved differently. Comments such as "oh my vote doesn't really count" are the equivalent of quitting, and history has shown us that apathy and fatalism have usually led to tyranny and oppression. Freedom, like everything good, must be maintained after it is achieved.

This chapter's subtopics contain points to think about when considering this great responsibility we all have.

Avoid being a one-issue voter

It's important to remember that our charge is to vote for the best *available* candidate when choosing our elected officials. There are exceptions here and there, but by and large, voting for or against a candidate on the basis of a single issue is an unwise use of our ballot privilege. This type of vote usually stems from personal sentiment or overly strong feelings for one particular issue. As right as one may be on a given issue, it doesn't erase the fact that our government is made up of many individuals in many offices. The wise use of our vote entails extending our knowledge beyond our own pet issue to the whole range of duties of that particular office.

A good example of this would be abortion. I have heard of some who would not vote for a school board candidate, mayor, councilperson or other county or state office because the candidate was pro-abortion. In view of the fact that officials at these levels have no authority to make or change abortion law, that is not a wise use of one's vote—no matter how wrong abortion may be. It is vital to be informed not only of current issues, but also to be informed of how one's state, county and city government laws are set up so that we can tell exactly what a given government official can or cannot do. This is especially important during the campaign cycle as politicians are fond of making promises, (because they sound good, or appeal to certain one-issue constituencies), that they will be in no position to make good on if elected.

One of the best ways to make sure you're not a one-issue voter is to use a balanced scorecard approach. This method takes into account the applicable government responsibilities and matches them with the candidate whose positions and qualifications make that person the best for that particular office.

Here's one I use when deciding which candidate from my party to select during the campaign season for a congressional representative to the U.S. Congress. It consists of a simple set of criteria based on the Constitution and other good government principles, which are then ranked in order of importance. The candidate with the highest score gets my vote. Then I rate them on a scale of 1–10 depending on their rhetoric and how they answer questions. The 1–10 rating is important because of the fact that the media is not very discerning in helping us investigate a candidate, (outside of their scandals) and many times you won't be able to get a direct answer or position statement from the candidate for some of the criteria. That means that sometimes you'll have to rely on your feeling of how a candidate would deal with a given issue if elected.

Congressional Voting Scorecard

U.S. Congress	Candidate X	Candidate Y
Values tenth amendment	5	7
National Defense	9	5
Abortion	10	7
Balanced Budget	4	6
Total	28	25

This may seem a bit involved, but after doing it a time or two for each office, your criteria will form in your head as you find out about candidates during campaign seasons and the balanced approach will become part of your voting decision process.

Voting as an individual

Eternal salvation, just like civil rights, can only be achieved and possessed by individuals. It is true that we can and should help each other in achieving salvation and civil rights, but in the end, these things are our own personal responsibility. The Savior taught this principle in the parable of the ten virgins, when he told how the foolish virgins could not benefit by borrowing from the wise virgin's oil. The same goes with spiritual witness; no matter how strong the testimony of say, your father or spouse may be, you cannot ride that testimony into the celestial kingdom. You must develop and exercise your own. In like manner, hitching your political allegiances and fortunes to others based on the supposed strength of the group will not ensure your life, liberty, and pursuit of happiness. Belonging to parties and organizations is a wonderful way to be politically involved…until it replaces thinking and searching for truth.

A common misuse of our ballot privilege is using it to vote for benefits for any voting bloc, or special interest we may belong to or have sympathy for. This kind of vote became popular as government expanded. Politicians began promising money or other government benefits for certain groups of people. This is the very fault through which democracy's downfall was predicted: that once people could vote themselves money out of the treasury, the republic would then disintegrate into chaos and fighting over who got what.

Here are a few of the most prominent voting bloc interest groups that should not form part of our voting decisions:

<u>Class Warfare</u>

Envy is an insidious vice and should not be allowed to govern one's vote. When we let any politician start dividing us up into the poor, middle class, or the rich, and we vote for that candidate, we have given our tacit approval to set up a cannibalistic system of government. These politician "head-cannibals" get elected on the basis of who they mark as the fattest targets, ("the rich," "big business," SUV Owners, etc.), or what I call the 200-pounders. That may seem comfortable when one owns no business or is not rich, i.e., weighs 125 pounds amidst the 200-pounders. But the cannibal system doesn't worry about making more 200-pound people; it's just concerned with deciding which people to eat. The day always comes, though, when the 200-pounders have been consumed and the 100-pound people start voting to come get the 125 pounders. It's a vicious cycle that we must not participate in. Good government is good for *everyone*...not just the people of one income level or other defining characteristic.

Age

Social Security has created a large rift between retired people and those who are still working in their chosen professions. Politicians base entire platforms on this conflict of interest between the two because such a large chunk of the federal budget is spent on Social Security, (also because higher percentages of the elderly vote in most elections.) You have read what the brethren have said about this program. It must not be the principle issue upon which anyone bases his or her vote.

Race

Affirmative Action and other race-based laws are unconstitutional and no matter what race we are, we should be using our vote to abolish them. There are many politicians who shamelessly pander to members of various ethnic factions and whip up public sentiment against certain groups of people that they alone have decided are "persecuting" others. Legislation should be based on its right-ness or wrong-ness...not on the color of someone's skin.

Gender

Latter-day Saints do not believe that women should be paid less for the same work, or suffer any other type of inequality; however, gender-based legislation like Affirmative Action is not the solution to the problem. If we base our vote for a candidate on the basis of their gender, we are misusing the power of our vote and driving ourselves farther apart as a people.

Religion

One of the biggest political bogeymen the media has created has been that of the "Christian Right." Even though Latter-day Saints are not considered as part of the Christian Right, we do share many of the same values. The problems come when public policy and legislation are enacted that discriminate against one religious group in favor of another. We have seen this many times at various levels of government as some have been allowed to persecute the church through the legal system in the building of temples, or purchasing of property.

Another difficulty arises when people who have strong religious beliefs hold office and are persecuted for their beliefs instead of their public acts. John Ashcroft is a good example; his tenure as Attorney General of the United States has been exemplary, yet many of his detractors maintain that he would like to establish a theocracy simply because he holds Bible study and prayer groups among his co-workers at the Department of Justice. We must be strong champions of good people of all religions in public office.

<u>Demonization of big business</u>

No corporation should be able to skirt accounting laws or pollute the environment just because they are a large corporation. However, no large business should be penalized simply for being successful. Today's news is filled with references to "big oil," or "big fast food" as special interest groups try to get special laws passed, or bring lawsuits to drain profits from these companies. This is counter-productive to our economy and is promoted by appealing to the class warfare mentality. What must be taken into account is that there are relatively very few people in these large corporations that make big salaries or profits. On the contrary, the thousands of jobs provided by these businesses are one of their principle benefits to society. Most of the harm from these lawsuits and legislation is dealt out not to the big salaried employees, but to the regular employees in the form of lay-offs, and to the consumer in the form of higher prices. No politician should be able to make a career for him or herself by promising to prosecute companies simply for being successful.

Voting with the mind as well as the heart

It's always a challenge to balance these two forces when deciding one's vote. Sometimes a candidate is wrong on lots of issues, but our heart tells us that we should vote for that person anyway. Other times our heart convinces us that we dislike a given politician too much to vote for them even though he or she may be right on all the issues.

A good rule of thumb is to first discern if it's our heart favoring our own personal preferences for or against certain types of behaviors or characteristics; for example, where someone comes from, etc. Many people make voting choices because of the candidate's gender, accent, or some other personal trait that has little to do with how well that person would serve in the office. We were blessed with both thoughts and feelings…we should always be looking to balance the two so that we can be of one heart and mind in propagating good and righteous government.

Have the Brethren spoken?

In chapter 4 ("Politics from the Pulpit"), we learned that there are many political issues that the brethren have spoken about from the pulpit at General Conference. This makes it easier for us to make ballot box decisions on these issues because we have the mind and will of the Lord.

When it comes to those things the brethren may not have spoken about, we have not been left without guidance. We have the means necessary to make reasonable conclusions regarding how to vote on other issues because we have the scriptures and the divinely inspired Constitution (see chapter 13, The "Just and Holy Principles" of the Constitution) to help us make proper choices. Some try to blur that counsel by differentiating between legal, (or political), issues as opposed to purely moral issues. There are very few purely political or legal issues though...***ultimately, government is mostly about moral issues.***

- Whether or not we decide how to live our lives is a moral issue.
- Whether or not we are permitted to defend our lives is a moral issue.
- Whether or not some get to take other's property legally is a moral issue.
- Whether or not people and businesses all operate by the same rules is a moral issue.
- Whether or not our children are educated properly is a moral issue.
- Whether or not all are treated equally and fairly before the law is a moral issue.
- Whether or not future citizens inherit the same rights and freedoms we enjoy is a moral issue.

Since most government choices encompass morality it behooves us to seek the Lord's mind and will in our voting decisions by:

1. Searching the scriptures
2. Prayerfully considering what modern prophets and apostles have said
3. Reading the Constitution and the Federalist Papers

Voting As One

Imagine the kind of good men and laws we could observe to uphold if we learned the principles of the Gospel in relation to the principles of freedom in the Constitution and then all voted according to those principles! That is much different than lock step voting because we will not be taking a stand simply because others in our church have taken it; we will have come to the same conclusion by rallying around principles of righteous government. Remember the Prophet Joseph's statement:

> "When you get the Latter-day Saints to agree on any point, you may know it is the voice of God."
> Discourses of Brigham Young, 12:301, p.469

Politicians and policy makers would then learn those principles because they'd know that if they ran contrary to them they would face millions of Latter-day Saint voters at the ballot box. They would know that Latter-day Saint voters are not represented by some self-appointed "Reverend", to show up in the media making outrageous statements and pandering to special interest groups in order to pressure businesses and lobby the government. On the contrary, they would know that we cannot be bought and that we show up on election days to vote our convictions which are steady, consistent and do not change because of society's shifting winds.

I remember when President Hinckley appeared as a guest on the Larry King show in 1998. When asked by Mr. King what attracted people to the church, President Hinckley replied that the teachings of Christ were a solid anchor in troubled times that people could hold to, knowing that they wouldn't change with the whims of men. If we, as individuals, came to know and were anchored in those principles, think of the unshifting anchor we would be as citizens and voters. As President Taylor said, we could "act as a unit," and "operate as one" at the ballot box. Wise and honest men would come to know and depend on us to support them in their efforts to achieve good limited constitutional government. They would also know that we do not just pay lip service to those principles, but that we actually show up at the polls on all election days to back them up.

CHAPTER 12

▼

THE 21ST CENTURY'S GADIANTON ROBBERS

- Identifying Signs of a Secret Combination
- The Emergence of Today's Secret Combinations
- Communism
- Terrorism
- Gangs
- Shadows of Secret Combinations
- Defeating Secret combinations is an important part of defending the Constitution

Identifying signs of a secret combination

The way to identify any organization properly is to examine what it teaches and what it does, and secret combinations are no exception. Put another way, we should look at goals and methods. The Book of Mormon teaches that secret combinations use robbery and murder so that certain groups of people may protect each other in seeking power, riches and the triumph of evil:

> 22...Satan did stir up the hearts of the more part of the Nephites, insomuch that they did unite with those bands of robbers, and did enter into their covenants

*and their oaths, that they would protect and **preserve one another** in whatsoever difficult circumstances they should be placed, that they should not suffer for their murders, and their plunderings, and their stealings.*

*23 And thus **they might murder, and plunder, and steal, and commit whoredoms and all manner of wickedness,** contrary to the laws of their country and also the laws of their God.* Helaman 6:21,23

*And they were kept up by the power of the devil to administer these oaths unto the people, to keep them in darkness, **to help such as sought power to gain power,** and to **murder, and to plunder, and to lie, and to commit all manner of wickedness and whoredoms.***
Ether 8:16 (bold, author's)

Any organization that shares these methods or goals can be correctly identified as a secret combination. It becomes us as Latter-day Saints to be vigilant in identifying and combating our day's secret combinations.

The emergence of today's secret combinations

We're currently witnessing the same phenomenon that occurred in the Book of Mormon during the 70 or so years prior to the coming of the Savior; the emergence of secret combinations once evil nation-states have been defeated in conventional warfare.

Book of Mormon readers will remember that after Amalickiah and his "king-men" sought to overthrow the Nephite government they were routed by Captain Moroni's army under the Title of Liberty. After that defeat, they went over to the Lamanites to stir them up to attempt the same goal. This triggered a series of wars and conflicts that lasted approximately 16 years, (and twelve Book of Mormon chapters), in which Captain Moroni and the Nephite armies fought and defeated the invading Lamanites. At the end of the book of Alma, the reader is tempted to breathe a sigh of relief once the Lamanites were decisively defeated. But it didn't even take two years before a new threat loomed on the horizon—the Gadianton Robbers. The Nephites failed to recognize this new brand of evil masterminded by Kishkumen and Gadianton and ended up losing their free and democratic government. Because they returned to iniquity quickly after the battles were won, they were unable to perceive the Gadianton threat. They forgot that it was the Lord who had delivered them from the Lamanite armies, and that they would still need his help if they were to defeat this new enemy.

Communism

Now it is our turn in the Latter-days to witness and battle these various secret combinations. We have already seen the rise and much of the decline of the first secret combination to come out of World War II. Elder Bruce R. McConkie, discussing the 8th chapter of Ether in his book "The Millennial Messiah," wrote:

> *"**Next Moroni turns the key so that all who have ears to hear can understand what the secret combination is and can identify those who build it up.** "For it cometh to pass," he says, "that whoso buildeth it up seeketh to overthrow the freedom of all lands, nations, and countries." This is a worldwide conspiracy. It is now entrenched in many nations, and it seeks dominion over all nations. It is Godless, atheistic, and operates by compulsion. **It is communism**."* Bruce R. McConkie, The Millennial Messiah, p.66 (bold, author's)

The communist movement was/is dedicated to overthrowing democracy and the abolition of freedom of religion and property rights. Communism was defeated in part on the physical battlefield; the rest of the campaign was won because good and righteous people worked through a variety of political means to conquer it. (No disrespect intended toward those brave men and women who died in Korea, Vietnam or any of the other conventional wars against communism.) Some of these warriors were members and leaders of the Church of Jesus Christ of Latter-day Saints, (see chapters 4 & 6). In our day we have been blessed to witness most of the world's communist regimes being relegated to "the ash heap of history," with the few remaining either dying on the vine or transitioning to democracy. As a result, millions have been liberated not just politically, but also spiritually and are now enjoying the opportunity to hear the Gospel. However, that "peace dividend" from winning the Cold War gave way to a complacency that ignored the next secret combination threat waiting eagerly in the wings.

Terrorism

Terrorism as we know it today, (though it became much more of an issue on September 11th, 2001), began its spread in the 1970's when terrorists began killing innocent people instead of assassinating leaders or blowing up government buildings. Terrorists' methods are murder and their goals are domination over others' freedom along with the plunder of their substance. Today's terrorist organizations are much more like the Gadianton band in Book of Mormon times because they either infiltrate countries or hide in the mountains of some remote corner of the world.

Al Quaeda and the followers of Osama Bin Laden do both. There are some who hide in the mountainous regions of the Afghanistan-Pakistan border just like those robbers of old:

> "...the Gadianton robbers, who dwelt upon the mountains...did infest the land; for so strong were their holds and their secret places that the people could not overpower them; therefore they did commit many murders, and did do much slaughter among the people.
> (3 Nephi 1:27)

Fortunately in our day we have better military means of fighting them, but even so, it is notable that, (at the writing of this book), almost three years after the invasion of Afghanistan, coalition forces are still engaged in finding and rooting out these mountain-dwelling terrorists.

Islamo-fascist terrorists come to live and work among us so that they can hijack planes, plant bombs and otherwise work their methods of terror. What is more insidious about them though is that they provide cover for the people who fund their crimes. There are rulers in the Middle East who know they cannot compete on the battlefield, so they are sponsoring this cowardly method of warfare in an attempt to destroy democracy and Christianity. Though "the war on terror" is a good way to describe the overall effort against Islamo-Fascism, it's vital to remember that we are not engaged in a conventional war because *terror is a method, not an enemy.* There are no countries with the name "The National Republic of Terror", because terrorists and the countries that harbor them know that if they were to declare themselves as such, they would be defeated by the United States' military. Because of their dishonest way of waging war we must determine which countries are the sponsors of terrorism and then treat them as enemies. This is what is meant by "the Bush doctrine" and it is a righteous way of waging war against the secret combinations of today and is worthy of the support of every defender of the Constitution.

The face of Islamic terror resides not only in Al Quaeda, but also in Hezbollah, the Palestinian Liberation Organization (PLO), Hamas and a number of others. They all fit the definition of a secret combination because they all employ murder to pressure western powers (or Israel) to abandon territory and property to them so that they can possess it. For all their religious posturing, their demands are the same as the Gadianton terrorists of old. Giddianhi, the chief of the Gadianton Robbers wrote an epistle to Lachoneus the chief judge; its demands sound eerily similar to modern terrorist rants:

> "And I write this epistle unto you, Lachoneus, and I hope that ye will **deliver up your lands and your possessions,** *without the shedding of blood, that this* **my people may** *recover their rights and government, who have dissented away from you because of* **your wickedness in retaining from them their rights of government,** *I will avenge their wrongs. I am Giddianhi."*
> (3 Nephi 3: 10)

Notice that the robbers wanted all the Nephites' possessions along with the right to rule over them. In the end, that's usually the major goal of those who want to rob the free of their liberty, and that's what today's terrorists are after. Like Satan, they cannot enjoy their own happiness unless it involves making someone else miserable. They are unable to reproduce the fruits of moral agency, (happiness and prosperity), so they seek to destroy it. They have no plan to build or create anything, merely the desire to tear down what others have created. People who employ the methods of secret combinations of terror need not be understood, they need to be defeated.

Gangs

President Boyd K. Packer has identified gangs as secret combinations.

> *"When Moroni was translating the twenty-four gold plates, he interrupted his narrative to speak directly to us in our day. He told of the Gadiantons and their bands (in our day we would call them gangs)"*
> "On the Shoulders of Giants," Brigham Young University J. Reuben Clark Law Society Devotional, February 28, 2004

Today's gangs are only interested in the plunder. They do not seek to govern, (unless it is their own "turf.") Gangs, like terrorists, rely on their victims' fear so that they can be more easily robbed. It behooves us to do all we can to aid law enforcement in eradicating the scourge of gangs, as well as exposing any who may exist in our own communities.

Shadows of secret combinations

There are organizations in existence today that qualify in part as secret combinations because they share some of the goals and methods even though they do not fit all of the identifying points. Most are political, the rest are focused on one particular special interest or another. In identifying these groups it is important to remember that they should not be considered on a level with communist or terrorist groups, but should certainly not be given moral equivalence with law-abiding, Constitution-honoring organizations.

The American Civil Liberties Union (ACLU)
This once-great organization used to work for equality and civil liberties for all Americans, and still does champion some worthwhile causes. Unfortunately it has become a left-wing apparatus for promoting taxpayer funded on-demand abortion rights, legalizing same-sex marriage, and other immoral and anti-constitutional measures. Though their methods may be legal, the ACLU is certainly engaged in helping people "*commit all manner of wickedness and whoredoms.*"

Some Environmental and Animal Rights Groups
Earth First, The Earth Liberation Front, People for the Ethical Treatment of Animals (PETA), SHAC and many others have had members convicted of one or more acts of terrorism such as assault, battery, or property destruction that ended in the killing of innocent people. Their leaders, even if not involved in the acts themselves, certainly condone the methods, which can definitely be termed as "protect[ing] and preserv[ing] one another in whatsoever difficult circumstances they should be placed, that they should not suffer for their murders, and their plunderings, and their stealings."

The Council on Foreign Relations
This multi-national body has set itself up as an authority to help governments make foreign policy decisions. Little is known though, about its true agenda and government philosophy.

Some Foundations
There are many foundations established by many great and wonderful people and these foundations perform many wonderful and charitable works. The Deseret Foundation is one such organization. There are others however, like the Ford Foundation, Pew Charitable Trusts, Tides Foundation, and many others that routinely obscure the sources of their tax-exempt millions in order to make it difficult, if not impossible, to discern how the funds are actually being used.

In practice, these foundations behave less like philanthropies and more like money-laundering operations, taking money from other foundations and spending it as the donor requires. This is called "donor-advised giving," and provides public relations insulation for the money's original donors. By using one of these foundations to funnel its capital, a large public charity can indirectly fund a project with which it would prefer not to be directly identified such as abortion, or homosexual rights. Latter-day Saints should take the time to inform themselves about any organization or foundation to which they wish to contribute time, talents, or money to ensure that they are not involved in anti-Constitutional causes or are otherwise violating tax statutes *"contrary to the laws of their country."*

Defeating Secret combinations is an important part of defending the Constitution

As the Savior was beginning his earthly ministry in Israel, the democratic Nephite government of laws and judges by King Mosiah was collapsing. The seventh chapter of 3rd Nephi outlines the conditions that existed right before that downfall. Let us look for those that apply to our day:

> *And the people were divided one against another; and they did separate one from another into tribes, every man according to his family and his kindred and friends; and thus they did destroy the government of the land.* 3rd Nephi 7:2

Divisions along family, ethnicity, or other lines almost always precede the downfall of democracy. Today we are witnessing forces trying to split our country along a number of these lines; we see groups like the Rainbow Coalition trying to make it appear that the interests of blacks and whites conflict; we see politicians and organizations pitting the elderly against the young at the ballot box; and we can certainly observe those trying to divide the country along religious lines.

> *Now all this was done, and there were no wars as yet among them; and all this iniquity had come upon the people because they did yield themselves unto the power of Satan.* 3rd Nephi 7:5

We too have experienced no major wars for many years. In that time, Satan has made some of his greatest strides as we witness the declining morality, destruction of the family, and other spiritual decay in our country. This moral decline is the greatest threat to our freedom because righteousness is the base upon which our system of government rests. Elder Sterling W. Sill explained:

> *"In 1835 a French visitor, by the name of Alexis de Tocqueville, made a detailed study of our national operations. Later he wrote in his book: "America is great because she is good. And if America ever ceases to be good, she will cease to be*

great." This is a divine law that applies to all nations and to all individuals. But it applies particularly to us, because our extraordinary power and our extraordinary mission give us extraordinary responsibilities."
Sterling W. Sill, Conference Report, October 1970, p.76

And the regulations of the government were destroyed, because of the secret combination of the friends and kindreds of those who murdered the prophets. 3rd Nephi 7:6

Notice the final straw in the destruction of the Nephite democracy was that secret combinations destroyed the regulations of the government. Secret combinations are not just in the business of murdering and stealing; they are also obsessed with destroying the laws and regulations of righteous government, (that's why the ACLU qualifies as a secret combination.)

We're seeing that it becomes ever more important that we exercise righteous judgment in who and what we support. If we do not defend the Constitution against the many secret combinations intent on destroying it, we will be in danger of ignoring Moroni's warning:

Wherefore, O ye Gentiles, it is wisdom in God that these things should be shown unto you, that thereby ye may repent of your sins, and suffer not that these murderous combinations shall get above you, which are built up to get power and gain—and the work, yea, even the work of destruction come upon you, yea, even the sword of the justice of the Eternal God shall fall upon you, to your overthrow and destruction if ye shall suffer these things to be. (Ether 8:23)

CHAPTER 13

THE "JUST AND HOLY PRINCIPLES" OF THE CONSTITUTION

- Doctrine and Covenants Section 134—The Articles of Just and Holy Principles
- "Governments instituted of God"
- "Life, Property and Conscience"
- "The Civil Magistrate Should Restrain Crime"
- "The commission of crime should be punished according to the nature of the offense...
- "All men are bound to sustain and uphold the respective governments in which they reside, while protected in their inherent and inalienable rights...and that sedition and rebellion are unbecoming every citizen thus protected..."
- Mingling Religious Influence With Civil Government
- The Second Amendment

This chapter and the following two are intended as a three-part trilogy to help prepare to fulfill Joseph Smith's prophecy because in order to do that, we'll need to know:

> Chapter 13 The "Just and Holy Principles" of the Constitution (What we're defending)
> Chapter 14 "When the Constitution is on the Brink of Ruin" (How to recognize when it's at that point)
> Chapter 15 Bringing the Constitution Back from the Brink (Some ideas on how to save it)

Armed with that knowledge and strengthened in our conviction, we will be able to discern the signs of the times foreseen by brother Joseph:

> *"Even this nation will be on the very verge of crumbling to pieces and tumbling to the ground, and when the Constitution is upon the brink of ruin, this people will be the staff upon which the nation shall lean, and they shall bear the Constitution away from the very verge of destruction"*
> (19 July 1840, as recorded by Martha Jane Knowlton Coray; ms. in Church Historian's Office, Salt Lake City)

Doctrine and Covenants Section 134—The "Articles of Just and Holy Principles"

Just what *are* the "just and holy principles" of the Constitution?

There are many sources to read on this subject, but the scriptures are usually the best place to start. The heading of the 134th section of the Doctrine and Covenants says that it is "a declaration of beliefs regarding governments and laws in general." As you read it you will notice many of the plain and precious truths from the Declaration of Independence and the U.S. Constitution. Every verse in it, except one, starts out: "We believe..." That makes it very easy to consider this section as a kind of "Articles of Political Faith;" a series of statements that serve to remind us of what we believe. As we examine politicians and legislation we can view them through the lens of the beliefs laid out in this section of scripture.

The 134th section was written by Oliver Cowdery and W.W. Phelps and was then read and approved by the twelve in August 1835. The brethren had convened in conference in order to give final approval to publish the revelations received up to that point in time as "The Doctrine and Covenants." (Before then, the revelations received by the prophet had been published under the name "The

Book of Commandments") The reason for adding the 134th section as a scriptural statement on government was explained by Elder Joseph Fielding Smith:

> *"...the Latter-day Saints had been accused by their bitter enemies, both in Missouri and in other places, as being opposed to law and order. They had been portrayed as setting up laws in conflict with the laws of the country. This bitterness went so far that an accusation was brought against them, on one occasion in a Missouri court, of disloyalty because they believed that at some future time the Lord would set up his own kingdom which would supercede the government of the United States, and so believing that the time would come when such a kingdom would be established they were disloyal to the United States."*
> Joseph Fielding Smith, Church History and Modern Revelation, Vol 3, p.63

The 134th section of the Doctrine & Covenants is both a political manifesto and mission statement all rolled into one. It is vital that we grasp its principles and apply them to our latter-day politics.

"Governments instituted of God"

Though governments may appear to be largely man-made, God intended their principal purpose from the beginning—to secure the rights that will allow us to fulfill our earthly mission of agency, testing, and probation. The prophet John Taylor said:

> *"There are certain principles that are inherent in man, that belong to man, and that were enunciated in an early day, before the United States government was formed, and they are principles that rightfully belong to all men everywhere. They are described in the Declaration of Independence as unalienable rights, one of which is that men have a right to live; another is that they have a right to pursue happiness; and another is that they have a right to be free and no man has authority to deprive them of those God-given rights, and none but tyrants would do it. These principles, I say, are unalienable in man; they belong to him; they existed before any constitutions were framed or any laws made."*
> John Taylor, The Gospel Kingdom, p.306

Some types of government are better suited to securing God-given rights than others, and those are the governments we should seek to uphold. The first sentence of the first verse of section 134 does not make that crystal clear; Elder Joseph Fielding Smith gave us insight on how to better interpret that verse:

> *"We believe that governments were instituted of God for the benefit of man,"* might be more nearly correct if stated: *"A perfect government was instituted of God for the benefit of man."* The statement that governments, if this is interpreted to mean all governments, were instituted of God, may be questioned."
> Joseph Fielding Smith, Church History and Modern Revelation, Vol 3, p.63

I am not attempting to convince the reader that the scripture is incorrect; only that it was not received in the same way as the rest of the Doctrine and Covenants and as such can stand a little more light being shed upon it, (as Joseph Fielding Smith's comments demonstrate.) Elder Smith is drawing the distinction between governments that have God's approval and those that do not. In the eyes of heaven, all governments are not created equal. Obviously many cruel and dictatorial governments are not beneficial to man in securing their rights of life, conscience, and property and thus are not in line with God's will. Elder Smith's interpretation reinforces the fact that the patriarchal religious government that was instituted by God in the days of Adam is his preferred system. Failing that, governments should strive to carry out God's will in securing man's right to basic freedoms.

As we become involved in government and politics, an important thing is to remember is that the essential political covenant is between government and God, (not between the government and the governed), since *"he [God] holds men accountable for their acts in relation to them [governments]"*. (D&C 134:1) If we remember that important contract, then we will not just engage in "politics as usual," but see ourselves as accountable for helping to create saving conditions for our fellow man.

"Life, Property, and Conscience"

Life, property and conscience are the Doctrine & Covenants equivalent of "life, liberty and the pursuit of happiness" in the Declaration of Independence. These sets of terms refer to vital components needed by all God's children in order to work out their salvation.

"Life"

This term is the same in both because it is self-evident that life must be protected in order for us to be free agents here on earth. All who believe that only

God has the power to give and take life should vigorously oppose any government policy that does not protect the sanctity of life.

"Property/Liberty"

One of the reasons we came here to earth was to learn the correct way to treat our body and the proper way to dispose of physical possessions so as to subordinate the temporal to the spiritual. It is noteworthy that some of the 10 Commandments deal with property, both our own and that which belongs to others. Those that most readily come to mind are the eighth and the tenth commandments which tell us not to steal or covet. Elder Joseph L. Wirthlin taught the importance of this principle during the October 1944 General Conference:

> *"Labor was prior to capital, but property is the fruit of labor. Property is desirable and is a positive good to the world. That some should be rich shows that others may become rich and hence is just encouragement to industry and enterprise. Let not he who is houseless pull down the house of another, but let him work diligently and build one for himself, thus by example insuring that his own shall be safe from violence when built."*
> Joseph L. Wirthlin, Conference Report, October 1944, p.39

Other commandments that teach us about our possessions and their proper place in our lives are: "Thou shalt have no other gods before me," and "Remember the Sabbath day to keep it holy." These commandments help us put property in its rightful place among our priorities. We are not to worship our own property by making it an idol that takes priority over our Heavenly Father and Sunday is a day in which we're to cease worrying about and working for our possessions.

These are divine principles we should keep in mind when it comes to our political thinking on property rights. We should not support laws that legalize the taking of property that rightfully belongs to another, nor should we uphold programs that induce some to covet property yet to be earned by our fellow citizens. One of government's primary roles is to protect personal property. When we give government the authority to redistribute our money, we lose free agency, and with it, our accountability.

Freedom of Conscience and Pursuit of Happiness

Both the first verse of the 134th section of the Doctrine and Covenants and The Declaration of Independence make clear that the principal purpose of government is to secure the conditions necessary for happiness, *not* to guarantee happiness itself. That may seem obvious but it needs to be stated why government cannot make such a guarantee:

1. It's impossible to guarantee someone else's happiness.
2. Not everyone's idea of happiness is the same.

The United States government began its transition from guarantor of individual rights to provider of happiness somewhere in the 1930's when the "chicken in every pot and two cars in every garage" style of rhetoric became a popular way of making political promises. Implicit in that promise is the violation of individual property rights. Chickens must be raised, cars must be manufactured, and garages must be built; all by people who own the product of their labor. When the government starts promising education, health care, and jobs, it by definition assumes power over the lives, property, and conscience of its individual citizens. Once government infringes upon those God-given rights, it loses its divine stamp of approval.

One of my favorite scriptures is found in 2nd Nephi, chapter ten, verse 23:

"Therefore, cheer up your hearts, and remember that ye are free to act for yourselves—to choose the way of everlasting death or the way of eternal life."

Government should be in the business of ensuring an equal playing field…not guaranteeing the outcome of the game.

"The Civil Magistrate Should Restrain Crime"

In order to deter violation of one another's right to life and property; we should uphold laws and judges that properly restrain crime. It is not the job of the government to rehabilitate criminals, (that is the province of family, church and social organizations), but to create conditions whereby criminals are deterred from committing crime. The point at which restraining crime has gone too far is when basic rights are infringed.

"The commission of crime should be punished according to the nature of the offense…"

One of the reasons crime is not very restrained in our day is because criminals do not fear the consequences of committing their crimes. Criminal sentencing has reached an all-time lenience that does not punish criminals, and as a result shamefully disregards the protection of the innocent. The average murderer spends between 4–8 years in prison; the average rapist spends 2–4 years incarcerated, and the average thief spends between 6 months to two years in a jail cell. What happens after that is a direct result of the crime not being punished according to the nature of the offense:

> *"In 1991, 45 percent of state prisoners were persons who, at the time they committed their offense, were under conditional supervision in the community—either on probation or on parole," states a report by the U.S. Justice Department. "Based on the offense that brought them to prison, the 162,000 probation violators committed at least 6,400 murders, 7,400 rapes, 10,400 assaults, and 17,000 robberies, while under supervision in the community an average of 17 months." Based on the offense that brought parolees back to prison, these 156,000 offenders committed at least 6,800 murders, 5,500 rapes, 8,800 assaults and 22,500 robberies, while under supervision in the community an average of 13 months,"*
>
> "Probation and Parole Violators in State Prison" (Survey of State Prison Inmates, 1991)
>
> U.S. Department of Justice, Office of Justice Programs, Bureau of Justice Statistics
>
> Special Report, August 1995, NCJ-149076

It is just and fair for us to give strong support to right-thinking attorneys general, judges, legislators and law enforcement officials.

"All men are bound to sustain and uphold the respective governments in which they reside, while protected in their inherent and inalienable rights…and that sedition and rebellion are unbecoming every citizen thus protected…"

Some have interpreted this passage in such a way as to suggest that the American revolutionaries and the founding fathers were not inspired. That is not the case. America's revolution was prophesied by Nephi, (1Nephi 13:17–19), and sanctioned by God:

> *"And for this purpose have I established the Constitution of this land, by the hands of wise men whom I raised up unto this very purpose, and redeemed the land by the shedding of blood."*
>
> D&C 101: 80

Our upholding of government is conditional upon its protecting the "inherent and inalienable rights" of its citizens. That of course does not mean that every time a right is violated we are given tacit permission by God to rebel. Latter-day Saints in Ohio, Missouri, and Illinois were certainly not protected by the government, yet Joseph Smith did not lead a revolution. He did what we should do: use peaceful means to right the wrongs and prevent them from recurrence by appealing to elected officials and by running for office. The purpose for including the 134th section in the Doctrine and Covenants was to let others know that Latter-day Saints respect the rule of law and will work within constitutionally approved methods to bring about justice and needed change.

Mingling religious influence with civil government

Verse 9 states:

> *"We do not believe it just to mingle religious influence with civil government, whereby one religious society is fostered and another proscribed in its spiritual privileges, and the individual rights of its members, as citizens, denied."* (D&C 134:9)

This is a clear affirmation of the first amendment to the U.S. Constitution, which reads: "Congress shall make no law respecting an establishment of religion, or prohibiting the free exercise thereof…" A common misinterpretation of this amendment has come to be accepted in our day, called the doctrine of "separation of church and state." This concept is not found in the Constitution but in a letter written by Thomas Jefferson to the Danbury Baptist Association in 1801, and has come to be interpreted that the Constitution bars any contact between religion and any part of government. This is absurd on its face. If the government is "we the people", and we the people are members of a religion, then religion will indeed touch government.

The correct way to understand this principle lies in the plain language of the founding fathers. The first sentence of the amendment says: "Congress shall make no law respecting an establishment of religion." The framers were keenly aware that the pilgrims came to America to escape the state-mandated Church of England so they could worship according to the dictates of their conscience. Thus the first amendment to the Constitution means that the government may not establish, or set up a state religion as England did. It does not mean that there can be no nativity scene in the town square. It does not mean that prayers cannot be said in school. And it does not mean that the words "under God" may not appear in the pledge of allegiance. Secular forces are working hard to ensure that

America is free of all religious influence. In fact, that is the religion of the secularists...that there can be no religion in public places or in political and government discourse. Our title of liberty is to defend not only our own right to practice our religion, but the rights of all other religions to practice theirs as well.

The second amendment

In Section 134, verse 11 we read:

> "...we believe that all men are justified in defending themselves, their friends, and property, and the government, from the unlawful assaults and encroachments of all persons in times of exigency, where immediate appeal cannot be made to the laws, and relief afforded." (D&C 134:11)

That verse is a modern day version of this verse in the Book of Mormon:

> *"Now the Nephites were taught to defend themselves against their enemies, even to the shedding of blood if it were necessary; yea, and they were also taught never to give an offense, yea, and never to raise the sword except it were against an enemy, except it were to preserve their lives."* (Alma 48:14)

Self-protection in the face of danger, whether with a sword or a firearm is something we believe in firmly. In the next two chapters I will touch on how this essential right is currently in danger along with some ideas on what we can do to protect it.

Conclusion

There are more just and holy principles besides the ones mentioned in this chapter. I would encourage us all to do as President Benson counseled in his opening remarks in the October 1987 General Conference commemorating the 200th anniversary of the ratification of the United States Constitution:

> *"Have we read The Federalist papers? Are we reading the Constitution and pondering it? Are we aware of its principles? Are we abiding by these principles and teaching them to others?"*

Chapter 14

"When the Constitution is on the Brink of Ruin"

- Fraying Constitutional Threads
- The Tenth Amendment & Federalism
- Legislative Abuse—Federal Agencies and Bureaus
- Gerrymandering
- Judicial Overreach
- The Second Amendment
- Entitlements
- Divided We Cannot Stand

Fraying Constitutional Threads

Speaking at general conference in October 1942, President J. Reuben Clark, Jr., a member of the First Presidency, asked a question regarding Joseph Smith's prophecy about the Constitution:

> "You and I have heard all our lives that the time may come when the Constitution may hang by a thread. I do not know whether it is a thread or a small rope

by which it now hangs, but I do know that whether it shall live or die is now in the balance.

I have said to you before, brethren, that to me the Constitution is a part of my religion...It is a part of my religion because it is one of those institutions which God has set up for His own purposes...because under no other government in the world could the Church have been established as it has been established under this government."

That's a strong message for us today—in 1942 one of our greatest constitutional scholars said that he didn't know if the Constitution hung by a rope or a thread, *but he was busy asking himself the question.* Some who are alive today might say: "it must have hung by a rope, because he asked the question over 60 years ago and the Constitution is obviously still holding on." I would only suggest that the thickness of the rope is perhaps not as important as the rate of the fraying, and constitutional fiber snapping is definitely accelerating! Most of the fraying constitutional threads discussed in this chapter had already started coming unwound by the 1940's, which gives us an even more urgent reason to gather together and save it from destruction as more and more fibers snap at an ever quickening pace.

The Tenth Amendment & Federalism

When we are taught in civics about the Constitution's checks and balances we are usually only taught about those checks between the executive, legislative and judicial branches. The great vision of the founding fathers encompassed more than just those three safeguards. There are many checks and balances built into the Constitution. The principle of federalism, best expressed in the 10th amendment, is one of the Constitution's most important reins on government power and it has virtually disappeared from today's government framework.

Federalism is best defined as "a union of states in which sovereignty is divided between a central authority and the member state authorities." In other words, there are some functions the big federal government is in charge of and the rest are performed by each individual state of the union. The 10th amendment draws that line between which specific tasks should be performed by the federal government and which are to be taken care of by the individual states:

> Amendment X
> *The powers not delegated to the United States by the Constitution, nor prohibited by it to the states, are reserved to the states respectively, or to the people.*

The founding fathers in their wisdom knew that power-grabbing was a natural outgrowth of government, so they ratified the tenth amendment to remind us that any function not outlined in the Constitution belongs under the jurisdiction of each individual state of the union.

Here is a nearly comprehensive list of the constitutional duties and functions for which the federal government is constitutionally responsible. (*I've left out some outdated, minor, or internal functions like granting letters of marque, establishing postal roads, impeachments, keeping legislative records, and operating the territory of Washington D.C.*)

- National defense (declare war, raise armies, maintain militia & navy)
- Make treaties with foreign countries
- Lay (decide how much) and collect taxes
- Coin (mint) money, borrow money and regulate foreign commerce
- Establish immigration laws
- Establish post offices and copyright laws
- Establish federal courts in which to try federal crimes
- Make laws concerning interstate commerce and law enforcement
- Run federal elections/conduct census every ten years
- Admit new states into the union
- Indian affairs
- Establish a supreme court as a court of final appeal

Not a very long list is it? That's exactly what the founders intended.

Now here's just a *partial* list of functions that are run completely, (by granting or withholding of tax monies), by Washington D.C. that are nowhere found in the Constitution:

- Education
- Welfare
- Healthcare (Medicare/Medicaid)
- Retirement Pension—i.e., Social Security

- Environmental Protection
- Regulating farming and agriculture (USDA)
- Regulating food and drugs (FDA)
- Operating arts funding (NEA, National Endowment for the Arts)
- Regulating energy/electricity (DOE, Dept. of Energy)
- Operating home building and loan functions (HUD)
- Regulating transportation (DOT, Dept. of Transportation)
- Regulating employment law (Dept. of Labor)
- Establishing laws over radio and television (FCC)
- Natural disaster management
- Regulating railroads (Federal Railroad administration)
- Regulating fishing and wildlife services
- Geological surveying and mining
- Operating a home mortgage business (Govt. National Mortgage Assoc.)
- Operating museum and library services
- Space Exploration
- Science and research
- Ocean Management
- Peace Corps/Americorps
- Regulating and loaning money to small businesses
- Public Television/National Public Radio
- Making handicapped and disability laws
- Regulating telephone companies and other communications systems

That's quite a list of tenth amendment violations and it is by no means complete. If I were to make a comprehensive list of all the non-constitutional functions currently administered by the federal government it would fill multiple books as long as this one!

Caveat

In reading this list, please do not think that I am advocating that none of these issues be dealt with by government. We as a society need to be very concerned with education, welfare and taking care of the health of our citizens, but we should do it constitutionally, which means that *these duties should be taken care of by each individual state, not by a far-off yet ever-reaching federal government.* It is vital to the proper growth and development of our nation as a whole that functions are divided between federal and state governments. The founders knew that each state would be an individual political market that could judge its elected officials. If state officials abused their power, its citizens would have the freedom to either remove them or move to other states, or work to make the necessary changes at the state level. As it is today injustices are remedied much more slowly than needful because massive federal programs become entrenched bureaucracies whose mistakes are much more difficult to eradicate.

The founders never intended for citizens in North Dakota to pay for the regulation of ocean management or for people in Hawaii to pay for federal railroad administration. (Some might say that the founders could not have had such intentions since Hawaii's admission into the union was still 172 years away!) I would posit that the framers knew about power and its abuse and they set up a near perfect system for spiritual and economic growth by dividing duties as close to the local level as possible. James Madison, the Father of our Constitution, summed up the American concept of federalism well in the Federalist Papers #45:

> *"The powers delegated by the proposed Constitution to **the federal government are few and defined.** Those which are to remain in the State governments are numerous and indefinite. The former will be exercised principally on external objects, as war, peace, negotiation, and foreign commerce; with which last the power of taxation will, for the most part, be connected. The powers reserved to the several States will extend to all the objects which, in the ordinary course of affairs, concern the lives, liberties, and properties of the people, and the internal order, improvement, and prosperity of the State."*

Legislative Abuse—Federal Agencies and Bureaus

The Constitution assigns the law-making function to the legislative branch, but that is not how most laws are written and passed today. In the previous section I listed a number of the agencies that reside in the executive branch. This creation of federal agencies began in 1887 with the creation of the Interstate Commerce Commission (ICC), and then accelerated dramatically during the Roosevelt years as congress discovered that it could not possibly write all the specific laws pertaining to the multitude of federal agencies it had created. This "alphabet soup" of agencies grew rapidly with the FDIC, TVA, WPA, SSA, and many more, which has now grown into a endless list. This is unconstitutional because the executive branch has no law-making authority, yet the president appoints the heads of these agencies that write "rules" which have the effect of law. The Constitution says that laws are to be written and passed by congress and then sent to the President for approval or veto. The framers wrote the Constitution so that lawmakers would be accountable to voters, but today unaccountable bureaucrats write many of our laws.

We are left with a legislative process that has been rendered largely unconstitutional. Congress passes laws that are neither complete nor detailed, after which the corresponding federal agency "interprets" the law by writing additional specific regulations which then have the effect of law. *"The Federal Register"* is a gigantic volume of regulations that Congress has not voted on, but has the force of law (in 1935 the Federal Register, numbered 4,000 pages, it now numbers approximately 70,000 pages). These regulations must be meticulously scrutinized by businesses, property owners, and others who risk fines, (or worse), for running afoul of some obscure requirement. This unconstitutional legislation has also served to corrupt the practice of law, which will ultimately have the same effect on our society as it had on the ancient Nephite democracy:

> ...they had altered and trampled under their feet the laws of Mosiah, or that which the Lord commanded him to give unto the people; and they saw that their laws had become corrupted, and that they had become a wicked people...
> Helaman 4:22

Here's an example of this unconstitutional process and how it affects all of us:

The Clean Air Act, (passed in 1990), and other environmental laws contain language directing the EPA to "protect public health with adequate margins of safety" and don't mention whether the cost of such protection should be taken into account. After many hours of research I've concluded that neither side (industry or environmental) really knows how much this regulation has cost small business owners, (i.e., us consumers), simply because these regulations are so numerous and so open to interpretation that it's impossible to determine.

Here are just a few programs that the EPA has decreed that small businesses must institute:

- Controlling Ground Level Ozone (Smog)
- Reducing Emissions of Toxic Air Pollutants
- Preventing Accidental Release of Hazardous Chemicals
- Protecting the Upper Ozone Layer from:
  - Class I substances, which are the most damaging to the ozone layer and include 15 kinds of chlorofluorocarbons (CFCs), as well as halons, carbon tetrachloride and methyl chloroform.
  - Class II substances, known collectively as hydrochlorofluorocarbons or (HCFCs), which are less harmful to the ozone layer.
- Fleet Vehicle Controls: Beginning in 1998, fleet vehicles in 22 of the more polluted urban areas will be required to use clean burning fuels, or to purchase new cars, trucks or vans that emit virtually no pollution.

And there are hundreds more than these I've listed!

Imagine you're running a small business like a hardware store and how much it would cost you to make sure you're not running afoul of any of these multitudinous regulations! You'd have to pass those costs on to your customers in order to keep making a profit. Imagine how much more you as a consumer of small businesses (like hardware stores) have had to pay for any number of goods and services…all because of these regulations that have never been voted on by the officials we elected.

Caveat

After reading this example, some might say that since I'm speaking against the Environmental Protection Act that I favor dirty air and water. *(That would be a good example of "Attacking Motives spin," see chapter 8)* I am not in favor of polluting the environment. I advocate taking care of pollution by obeying the Constitution and letting the citizens of each state lobby their respective governments to make sure businesses are not polluting. Then state lawmakers who are familiar with the particular challenges of each state will be obligated to carry out that charge. Environmental concerns in Alaska are much different than those in Georgia and they should be addressed by the citizens of their respective states who know them best.

The most startling aspect of all these bureaus, agencies and volumes of regulation is how different this country's national government has become. The subtle growth of government has slowly eradicated constitutionally erected limits and is now a huge, self-perpetuating bureaucracy. Elder Boyd K. Packer gave an excellent description of this unconstitutional phenomenon some years ago:

> *"The bigger the government becomes the more lost we are as individuals. Somehow, always under the notion that our rights are being protected, webs are combined with threads, and threads are added to strings, and strings are fashioned into cords, and cords into ropes, and ropes into bonds."*
>
> *An excellent example of how things can get tangled up is the regulation issued under Title IX of the Education Amendments Act of 1972. The intent of that act was to prevent sex discrimination in federally assisted educational programs. As passed by Congress, Title IX was stated in twenty-seven words.*
>
> *The Department of Health, Education and Welfare, charged with its enforcement, published extensive regulations to enforce those twenty-seven words in Title IX. The regulations put together at sublevels in the bureaucracy amounted to about 20,000 words!*
>
> *Those who made these interpretations are neither known to be representative of the general feelings of the public, nor to understand the far-reaching effect of the regulations. Those 20,000 words of regulation are now being vigorously applied as law. They involve issues that Congress neither acted upon nor intended."*
>
> *Some of the results must be termed as preposterous: others of them surely must be unconstitutional.*

Boyd K. Packer, "The Equal Rights Amendment," Ensign, Mar. 1977, p. 6

Gerrymandering

The House of Representatives is often referred to as "The People's House" since its composition is based on each state's population and whose members serve comparatively short two year terms. It was designed like that by the founding fathers so as to be the most responsive to the voters. Citizens need to be able to send clear messages with their vote so the members of this important legislative body know their will. There should be a healthy amount of turnover in the House of Representatives, but this is not the case. This responsiveness has almost disappeared because of gerrymandering.

The term "gerrymander" was coined in honor of the congressman who started this questionable practice, a representative of the State of Massachusetts named Elbridge Gerry. He was the first to draw a congressional district in an odd shape so that more voters from his party lived in that district, thus ensuring his election (the district map's shape looked like a salamander, hence the name Gerrymander.") Due to greater technological and demographic prowess gerrymandering has been honed to a fine art and continues today, virtually guaranteeing the outcome of congressional elections in favor of the party in power when lines are drawn. In 2002, 80 percent of the 435 U.S. House races were won by margins of 20 percent or more. Only 38 races were even remotely competitive, with a margin of 10 percent or less separating the winner from the loser. Hard to believe when the country was split nearly 50–50 in the presidential election two years earlier!

This is a true and grave danger to the Constitution. If the House of Representatives continues to be perceived as unresponsive and unchangeable, voters will see little point in going to the polls just to re-elect incumbents. Once voters disengage, we run the danger warned of by the prophet Mosiah where an unrighteous minority chooses the direction of the country.

Judicial Overreach

The judicial branch was created as an important check on executive and legislative power; that's why judges are appointed, as opposed to elected, thus ensuring the fairest, most non-political judgment on legal issues. The judiciary though was destined to be the weaker branch because of the very fact that they were appointed, usually to life terms, and as such were less responsive to the will of the people. The judiciary has also mistakenly become the final arbiter of what is constitutional. I say mistaken, because it is "We the people" who make that decision through our elected representatives. The most egregious constitutional departure of our judiciary today is that instead of interpreting law, some judges are writing law. That's why the term "judicial tyranny" is popping up in the national discourse. Here are a couple of examples of how these judicial abuses are bringing the Constitution nearer the brink of destruction…

The First Amendment

The most egregious judicial overreach has been in first amendment interpretation. This amendment was intended to ensure that the government did not establish a state sponsored religion citizens would be required to join. The first amendment was never intended to completely separate government from religion. It was to ensure that any and all religions received equal treatment from the government so that everyone may enjoy freedom of conscience. Today the federal judiciary is a launching pad for attacking religious freedom. It is the tool being used by secular forces to accomplish things like eliminating the words "under God" from the pledge of allegiance, an effect never intended by the founders.

Making instead of interpreting law

The Supreme Court, in making itself the final judge of what is constitutional, has forced some horrible judgments on the country:

> 1857—Dred Scott: The Supreme Court rules that slavery is constitutional
> 1973—Roe v. Wade: The Supreme Court rules that abortion is constitutional
> 1978—University of California Regents v. Bakke: The Supreme Court rules that it's constitutional to discriminate on the basis of race.

These are matters much too important to be left to nine people virtually unaccountable to voters. The tenth amendment is a check and balance that can many times be employed against judicial overreach. In the case of abortion, it's easy to figure out where the decision should be made. The Constitution says nothing about reproductive rights; therefore it is an issue to be decided at the state level (which is how it was decided until 1973.)

Just as with other constitutional abuses, the principle being violated by today's judiciary is the concentration of too much power in the hands of too few. The ultimate bulwark against tyranny is the judgment of a righteous people. I cite again the wise words of Mosiah:

> *26 Now it is not common that the voice of the people desireth anything contrary to that which is right; but it is common for the lesser part of the people to desire that which is not right; therefore this shall ye observe and make it your law—to do your business by the voice of the people.*
> *27 And if the time comes that the voice of the people doth choose iniquity, then is the time that the judgments of God will come upon you; yea, then is the time he will visit you with great destruction even as he has hitherto visited this land."*
> Mosiah 29:26–27

The Second Amendment

> *"...the right of the people to keep and bear arms shall not be infringed"*

The founding fathers knew that an unarmed people would be subject to tyranny by runaway government. That's why this amendment occupies the number two spot in importance in the Bill of Rights. The first freedom is that of conscience and expression, after that comes the right to defend the first freedom. The freedom to keep and bear arms is in grave danger as there are currently thousands of federal laws infringing the people's right to keep and bear arms.

There are many organizations dedicated to wiping out this important freedom because firearms, just like cars and swimming pools, have the ability to kill as well as do good. Car accidents and accidental drownings easily kill many more children every year than firearms, yet there are no political movements to ban cars and pools.

I sincerely hope not, but it is possible that the Constitution will have to be defended by the use of arms. When and if that day comes, it will be necessary to emulate the ancient inhabitants of this land who came to the rescue of their government:

> *19 Moroni...went forth among the people, waving the rent part of his garment in the air...and crying with a loud voice, saying:*
> *20 Behold, whosoever will maintain this title upon the land, let them come forth in the strength of the Lord...*
> *21 And it came to pass that when Moroni had proclaimed these words, behold, the people came running together* **with their armor girded about their loins...**
> Moroni 46:19–21 (bold, author's)

It's reasonable to assume that these early American militiamen had swords and arrows in addition to their armor girded about their loins. We too have the same right...and duty.

Entitlements

Two of the most important commandments we're given relate to coveting or stealing of other's property. Today we live under a partly socialist system that promotes the entitlement mentality, which creates people who feel entitled to the fruits of other's labor. Ezra Taft Benson explained how this came to be in America:

> *"I have seen this great nation decline spiritually. What happens to a nation collectively is but the result of its citizenry departing from the fundamental spiritual and economic laws of God: making the Sabbath day a day of pleasure; individuals and businesses giving license to immorality; and politicians dignifying the coveting of others' possessions and property by stating, "We will take from the haves and give to the have nots." At first we resisted this philosophy; then consented;*

next, demanded; and now have legislated. Politically, we licensed coveting what others had earned!"
Teachings of Ezra Taft Benson, p.572–573

Notice how President Benson outlines the process of coveting as part of a chain that includes "departing from the fundamental spiritual and economic laws of God." Once we start taking from the Lord, (by violating laws regarding the day we're supposed to devote to His service), taking from one's fellowman becomes easier. Social Security is the principal culprit in our country's chain of covetousness. At present, the federal government pays out roughly 490 billion dollars, (about 21 percent of the federal budget) in Social Security benefits. Some have let themselves be deceived into believing that Social Security is a kind of pension system where one gets back what one has put into the system, plus interest, when that is not the case. It is in reality a ponzi scheme that rewards the early participants, leaving the later beneficiaries with nothing. In the beginning of Social Security's history, the real rate of return for the average single male retiring in 1940, according to Gareth Davis at the Heritage Foundation, was 114% a year. No pension system earns that kind of return. At present, the real rate of return for a single male born in 1960 and retiring in 2025 has collapsed to 0.97%. The end result of this program will be that the retirees in the beginning received much more than they put in; retirees today will receive much less than what their money should have earned, with those born today being the real losers. If Social Security is allowed to continue, today's youngest U.S. citizens will have to pay taxes so high that they will not be able to afford food, clothing and shelter. If we arrive at that point, I'm sure we'll se a new kind of Boston Tea Party as they will surely refuse to pay such confiscatory tax rates.

Social Security worked well in 1940 when there were 41 active workers for every one retiree receiving benefits…but now there are only about three active workers for every retiree. On top of that, benefits have been continually expanded, but at the same time the amount of benefits and the number of beneficiaries were expanding, life expectancy was also rising…to 77 years today from 63 years in 1940. More importantly, fertility rates have been dropping; in 1940, there were 2.2 children per female, but by 1998 there were fewer than two children (except for the 1950s when families had an average of more than three children). Accordingly, the number of workers supporting each Social Security dependent has dropped like a stone. After 2017 Social Security will be bankrupt and payroll tax rates will have to be dramatically increased with no money being put away for those paying into it. After that point retirees can only hope that their grandchildren will pay the high payroll tax rates needed to keep the system afloat.

Medicare and Medicaid have a similar future, (currently 19% of the federal budget—436 billion spent last year), except it involves the coercion of the medical profession in artificially fixing prices that doctors can charge for procedures in addition to a mountain of regulations that hinder the freedom of those involved in this vital profession.

It's not the statistics that make these entitlements wrong though. It's wrong because it's not just and holy to receive money and services from other citizens simply because enough people have voted that we can do so. Charity for the poor, the aged, and the sick is what we are here to learn. If we support the forcing of one person to do something good for another, then we have crossed over the aisle to Satan's way of thinking. Wasn't that his methodology? He wanted to get us all back to Heavenly Father's presence, (which is something very good), but he wanted to do it by taking away our free agency. In Satan's world the desirable ends justified the unrighteous means; we should not be lured over to his side by supporting legislation that does the same.

I am not advocating that those receiving or paying into Social Security should stop their participation. This program has grown over many years and we should not be yanking things away all at once. However, we must be able to identify the errors before we can fix them, and this is one of the most significant deviations from the Constitution that we have inherited. It behooves us now to vote for leaders who will implement some form of President Benson's plan to gradually eliminate entitlements. (See chapter 4, "Politics from the Pulpit.")

Divided We Cannot Stand

Our country's motto is "In God We Trust." We see it printed on all of our currency. That's an important thought to have continually before us. I'd like to focus for a moment though on our country's first motto: "E pluribus unum," which means "One from many," or "One from many parts." Thomas Jefferson, Benjamin Franklin and John Adams submitted this motto to congress along with their proposed design for the great seal of the United States. (The seal was rejected, but the motto was kept.) Due to the framer's great effort in getting the Constitution ratified this motto sought to highlight the new nation's unity as a country one in purpose, though composed of many different and distinct states. In retrospect, the ratification was a tremendous achievement; despite many diverse state interests from New Hampshire to Georgia the founding fathers were able to find enough agreement so as to establish a single federal government. The

Constitution's few errors, which lie in its treatment of blacks and native Americans, only existed because of that great struggle to unite the original thirteen colonies behind one common constitutional republic.

The founders knew that if states' and citizen's local interests became all-consuming, the union would break up and America would fragment into many smaller nation states (like Europe is today), and thus lose the great benefits that come through sacrificing some local interests for the sake of the growth and prosperity of the entire nation. That wisdom is being borne out today; witness the European Union and how they are trying to create greater prosperity by uniting the various small nation states under a common currency and legal system. Because of the founders' great vision we have not had to endure that difficult dynamic.

Destructive forces threaten our Constitution today by dividing the American people into politically warring groups and factions. All the various entitlements and preferences have served to create many "special interest groups" and "voting blocs" whose interests conflict because there are only so many tax dollars and government benefits to go around. The elderly vote for their social security and Medicare interests; minorities are urged to vote for whomever will guarantee discrimination in their favor, while the wealthy and middle class (the poor do not pay taxes) vote against each other so the tax code will be altered in their favor.

I cannot overemphasize how much this dividing of our people into interest groups is a danger to the Constitution. The Constitution originally designed government to be a guarantor of life, liberty, individual property and freedom of conscience—and that was all. For the first 150 years of our history our citizens looked to their families, churches and charitable organizations for retirement, welfare and other wants and needs. Then in the 1930's citizens were urged to look to government for all those things. We are reaching the end of that path and every day that the government spends in the re-distribution of money and services is another step closer to the brink of destruction of the United States Constitution. President David O. McKay saw the danger of an ever-expanding welfare state and warned:

> *"These revolutionists are using a technique that is as old as the human race,—a fervid but false solicitude for the unfortunate over whom they thus gain mastery, and then enslave them."*
>
> David O.McKay, *Statements on Communism and the Constitution of the United States* (Salt Lake City: Deseret Book Company, 1964) p.7

Conclusion

This chapter contains just a small number of the major areas where the Constitution has been attacked and degraded. There are many more for us to discover and discuss as a people. As President J. Reuben Clark said, whether the Constitution hangs by a rope or by a thread is an important question to be asking ourselves as part of our personal religious commitment. Are we personally involved in weakening it or strengthening it? We will not be able to answer that question in the positive unless we can first identify exactly where the Constitution is being attacked. We would do well to take personal inventory and ask ourselves the following questions posed by President Benson in his October 1987 general conference address "Our Divine Constitution":

> *"…Can we recognize when a law is constitutionally unsound? Do we know what the prophets have said about the Constitution and the threats to it?"*

Chapter 15

Bringing the Constitution Back from the Brink

- Specifics…
- Restoring the 10th Amendment
- Affirmative Action
- The House of Representatives
- The Senate
- The Executive Branch—Bureaus & Agencies
- Abortion
- Reining in the Judiciary
- Lawsuit Abuse (Tort Reform)
- Tax Reform

Specifics…

I don't know the specifics of exactly how the Constitution will be borne away from the brink of destruction. Will our Title of Liberty moment be as dramatic as Captain Moroni's, or will it be accomplished over time? Again, I do not know. I do know that we can prepare by beginning now to restore it in the same way as it has been eroded; little by little, initiative by initiative, by winning hearts and minds over to just and holy principles. Those who have gone about cutting our constitutional fibers have been cunning and ever so subtle. Take again the example of abortion. If pro-abortion proponents had just come out and said: "We need to make abortion legal," it never would have happened; instead, lawyers and judges invented the concepts of "a living constitution" and "penumbra." A "living constitution" turned out to be nothing more than a way to amend the Constitution in the courts instead of doing it by the will of the people as intended by the framers. A penumbra (which means a partial shadow), is a word used by judges to invent additional constitutional rights that do not actually exist in the Constitution. In the case of abortion, a "right to privacy" was invented so that the federal courts could then wipe out each individual state's abortion law so that the tenth amendment could not be applied.

This chapter is not meant to be a comprehensive list of things that will need to be done in order to restore the Constitution. Its purpose is to list the most urgent starting points and initiatives that can be undertaken in order to accomplish our charge in restoring the Constitution.

Restoring the 10th Amendment

This amendment has been violated so much that restoring it will consist in getting many of the large federal government programs, like Social Security, Medicare, Aid to Dependent Families (welfare), etc. shifted to the state level. It's important to remember that we do not oppose helping the poor, sick, or elderly, but that we do not believe that violating the tenth amendment by the creation of massive federal programs is the answer either. The following are programs and entitlements that will need to be handed back to the states in order to restore the 10th amendment.

Education
Ezra Taft Benson taught:

> *"The phrase federal aid to education is deceptive and dishonest. What is really meant is "federal taxes for education." The federal government cannot "aid" education. All it can do is tax the people, shuffle the money from one state to another and skim off its administrative costs from the top. Only the people can aid education. They can do it safer, faster, and cheaper within their local communities than by going through the middleman in Washington. Federal taxes for educa-*

tion means federal control over education. No matter how piously the national planners tell us that they will not dictate policies to local school systems, it is inevitable that they will in the long run. In fact, they already are doing it."
Teachings of Ezra Taft Benson, p.298

We will need to support abolishing the federal Department of Education and having the money sent back to the states so the citizens of each state can work together to create the best educational program and learning environment for its children.

Environment
The Environmental Protection Agency will need to be disbanded and the tax money returned to those who paid it so that each individual state can deal with its own unique environmental protection needs.

Transportation
The Dept. of Transportation needs to cut back so as to only comply with its constitutional duty regarding interstate commerce. It should mainly be concerned with interstate highways and little else. The remaining billions in its budget need to be returned to individual taxpayers.

Farming/Department of Agriculture
Except for some interstate commerce oversight, federal involvement in farming, especially the subsidy program, will need to be phased out. The rights of corporations as equal players in our economy should be upheld; however, we must not punish, or put on unequal grounds, individuals and families who wish to grow food. The family farm as a backbone of our economic system must be restored. Ezra Taft Benson put it eloquently:

> *I am dedicated to freedom for the farmer. There are some politicians who will continue to farm the farmer—but a good administration will want the farmer to farm his own farm. My goal for agriculture has been stated many times. It is for an agriculture that is expanding, prosperous, and free—for the benefit of the entire American people.*
> Teachings of Ezra Taft Benson, p.652

All the Rest
There's no need to go on listing all the departments and programs currently run by the federal government that need to be returned to the states. Remember Elder Maxwell's quote from chapter six; taming big government will be a great challenge. It will lie principally in persuading people to take back power that has been abused and return it to the individual states.

Affirmative Action

This legalized discrimination must be abolished if all are to stand equal in the eyes of the law of the land. Who gets what jobs, and which students are admitted to which universities needs to be decided entirely upon merit. Making up for past wrongs and paying reparations will only further drive wedges between individual Americans. This well-intentioned but misguided program exists mostly due to the rejection of God's commandments to love our neighbors as we love ourselves. Elder Neal A Maxwell describes this deviation:

> *"Once we remove belief in God from the center of our lives, as the Source of truth and as a Determiner of justice, a tremendous vacuum is created into which selfishness surges, a condition which governments delight in managing. Trends become a theology.* **A religion of regulations emerges in which tens of thousands of regulations seek to replace the Ten Commandments.**
> **And with this secular religion comes a frightening insistence on orthodoxy, enforced by the withdrawal and bestowal of benefits.** *Such governments inevitably tend to enlarge taxes and to stunt their citizens."*
> Neal A. Maxwell, "The Prohibitive Costs of a Value-free Society," Ensign, Oct. 1978, p. 52 (bold, author's)

Affirmative action, i.e., hiring and admission quotas, can and should be done away with in one motion. There is no reason to prolong this injustice.

The House of Representatives

As discussed in the previous chapter, the "people's house" has been subverted from its original design as a large representative body to one that mostly serves party interests at the expense of the people it is supposed to represent. Gerrymandering has ensured that almost no change occurs in a legislative body that should be constantly changing in order to reflect the will of the people in a dynamic and progressive society.

There is an easy way to eliminate gerrymandering—return to the smaller congressional districts established by the founding fathers. The Constitution originally specified that there should be one house representative for every thirty thousand people in a given state. This formula was followed until the House of Representatives grew to 435 members at which point, in 1911, congress passed a law freezing the number at 435. Currently each congressional district has over 600,000 people in it! This makes it easy for congress to draw these odd-shaped districts so that incumbents can be re-elected with ease.

We wouldn't need to go back to 30,000 per district; a good number would probably be around 150,000. This would put the house membership between 1,900 and 2,000 members and would make districts very difficult to gerrymander. Think of the benefits that would accrue from returning to the type of representation prescribed by the Constitution:

- Districts would be truly representative.
- Campaigns would cost much less; connecting with 150,000 voters is much easier and cheaper than connecting with 600,000.
- The professional politician for life would become a thing of the past and the house would again be populated with "citizen legislators"
- The huge influence of lobbyists would go away. The large numbers of lobbyists and money it would take to influence a majority of the house would make their efforts more transparent and easy to combat.
- The massive flow of federal legislation out of Washington D.C. would slow to a trickle almost overnight as it would take much more effort to get federal laws passed (just as the framers intended.)

We have no need for a multitude of federal laws flowing from Washington D.C. because the Constitution was designed specifically so that most of the governing power lie with the states. Restoring the House of Representatives goes hand in hand in restoring the tenth amendment.

The Senate

To bring back the senate as envisioned by the Constitution means the repeal of the 17th amendment passed in 1913. Before that amendment's passage each state's legislators chose its senators which made for a truly great deliberative body. State legislators, who were accountable to the people for these decisions, chose senators and for the most part they appointed wise and thoughtful citizens to go to Washington. The way it is today with popularly elected senators, the senate is no longer a great deliberative body but one that has shirked its responsibilities in confirming judges, and otherwise has become a body of partisan panderers and pork spenders—mostly wasting taxpayers' time and money.

We are in desperate need of the return of famous senate debates such as those featuring great orators like Henry Clay, Daniel Webster and John Calhoun so that the senate can act in its true function as a check on both the Executive and the House of Representatives.

The Executive Branch—Bureaus & Agencies

As the tenth amendment is restored and unconstitutional federal programs and departments are either abolished or returned to the states, the alphabet soup of agencies run by the executive branch will need to be cut back considerably—especially in their ability to make regulation with the force of law. Congress will actually have to pass tax laws that are precise and objectively definable. It will no longer be able to pass tax brackets, guidelines and exceptions, then hand the whole mess off to the IRS for interpretation and further rule/law making.

The federal government will need to get out of the business of regulating and taxing the communications industries, i.e., telephone and other communications services. The FCC should also be curtailed in its ability to regulate television and radio airwaves. Government's proper function in this regard is solely to determine interstate commerce aspects of airwaves, and to ensure adequate controls against obscenity and pornography.

The FEC (Federal Election Commission), along with most election laws, including and especially the unconstitutional McCain-Feingold campaign finance bill, will need to be struck down. A free press and free airwaves guarantee the people's unfettered right to choose their representatives and contribute to campaigns as they see fit. There are currently dozens of bureaus and agencies like the FEC that are unaccountable to the voters and in violation of the Constitution that will need to be done away with or cut back to their proper function. If I were to cover them all, this chapter would be as long as the entire book!

Abortion

In order to bring back the people's ability to decide this supremely important issue, Roe v. Wade needs to be struck down immediately and the power returned to each individual state for its citizens to decide.

Reining in the Judiciary

One of the biggest problems with the judicial branch today is that judges make law instead of interpreting it. Judges with political agendas are more and more common and obvious every day because they are appointed, not on the basis of their legal acumen, but because of their political leanings. We have seen this repeatedly as today's judicial appointment process has become more and more politicized. This is a direct result of senators being popularly elected instead of appointed by each states legislators and is exactly what the founders were trying to avoid.

The good news though is that this problem will disappear once the senate problem is fixed and current appointments retire. Senators elected by state legislatures will be less susceptible to the kinds of slander and spin currently passing for journalism today. Once we return to having constitutionally elected senators, they will again function in their appointed "advice and consent" role in confirming judges. There are other ways in which today's judicial branch abuses can be remedied. The checks and balances in the Constitution apply between all three branches, and the legislative has restraining power over judiciary, and possesses constitutional authority to restrict the extent of its jurisdiction. A non-gerrymandered, constitutionally elected congress will be equipped to exercise that authority.

The judiciary has been a big part of the problem in deviating from government's constitutional role regarding religion. Remember James E. Faust's great definition of the crux of this issue:

> *"The preeminence in the Constitution of the free exercise clause of the First Amendment has been overshadowed by the establishment clause and the free speech clause. In this I believe there has been a turning away from the intent of the Founding Fathers in the Supreme Court's interpretation of these clauses of the First Amendment."*
>
> James E. Faust, "The Constitution in the Tradition of the Founding Fathers," speech given at Utah State University, September 16, 2001

The legislature has the authority to define the court's jurisdiction so that the balance between free speech and religion can be restored. That authority must be used to return the judicial branch to its constitutional scope of activities and jurisdiction.

Lawsuit Abuse (Tort Reform)

The civil lawsuit process has been abused to the point that it has become a massive drain on society that has pushed insurance prices ever higher for all who pay for them. We have all heard of the high jury awards for spilling hot coffee on one's lap and other frivolous lawsuits. Honesty and responsibility dictate that we support tort (lawsuit) reform so that doctors can practice medicine freely and we as a people can be free from the high costs of this abuse. Restoring the civil lawsuit procedure to its rightful role should be done through supporting the legislature in using its capacity to define the jurisdiction of courts in their administration of the civil redress procedure.

Tax Reform

What is the largest expense facing the average American family today? It is not housing, food, clothing, or transportation. By far, the biggest expense for families today is taxes. Federal, state and local taxes consume about 40 percent of our family budgets. Taxes cost more than twice the amount for the next-largest expense (housing, 16 percent) and more than all the above-named items combined. It wasn't always this way though…

There was no income tax for the first 137 years of our country's existence. When the 16th amendment was introduced, The New York Times wrote in opposition: "When men get the habit of helping themselves to the property of others they are not easily cured of it." (The New York Times was a different paper then!) Unfortunately not enough people stood against the income tax because at the time it only applied to the rich (those who made over $1,000 a year), and the rates were low, (1%). So in 1913 the 16th amendment to the Constitution was ratified, mostly because voters were convinced that the income tax would never affect the average American—just the rich, along with the big corporations. Elder Joseph F. Merrill of the quorum of the twelve apostles expounded on the folly of that kind of thinking in General Conference, 1949:

> *"The popular idea is that these funds can be obtained from the rich and the big corporations—so that the majority of people can have the benefits without paying the cost. But nobody gets anything for nothing. Everybody shares the debt.* **Everybody pays taxes—direct or indirect.***"*
> Joseph F. Merrill, Conference Report, October 1949, p.37 (bold, author's)

One of the principal effects of higher taxes ended up being an assault on the family. Due to the tax burden today, many mothers are forced to work outside the home. That alone has contributed to our society's decline as much as any other government factor we could discuss. Up until the rapid expansion of the entitlement and welfare state that occurred in the 1960's, one income earner could support an entire family comfortably. This is just one way in which families are adversely affected by our current tax system.

The fix for this problem is not to re-set income tax rates and otherwise play with tax law, but to reform the federal government so that it doesn't spend so much. Another by-product of the constitutional restorations in this chapter will be the shrinking of the federal government, which in turn will be accompanied by a massive reduction in federal taxes. It is true that some burdens that were being unconstitutionally borne by the federal will be shifted to state governments and that state taxes will rise. However, each state will be able to make its decisions and hear its citizens arguments based on its own individual needs instead of being funneled into the massive federal system. The states will again begin to function as market indicators of good tax levels as citizens move to those states that are prudently run, and escape those states whose rates punish their residents.

Over 50 years ago, then 1st Counselor in the presiding bishopric, Joseph L. Wirthlin prophetically and accurately described our condition today if our tax system was allowed to continue its trajectory.

> *"Does history repeat itself? Yes. Today the term security is best defined in the promises of economic kings and politicians in the form of doles, grants, and subsidies made for the purpose of perpetuating themselves in public office, and at the same time depleting the resources of the people and the treasury of the nation. The word security is being used as an implement of political expediency, and the end results will be the loss of freedom, and temporal and spiritual bankruptcy. We have those among us who are calling for an economic king, and the voice of the king replies in promises wherein the individual is guaranteed relief from the mandate given to Adam, "In the sweat of thy face shalt thou eat bread." Disobedience to this mandate involves the penalty of loss of free agency and individuality, and the dissipation of the resources of the individual. These economic rulers have advocated, and do practice a vicious procedure called the "leveling down process," which takes from the man who has achieved and distributes to those who are not willing to put forth like effort. Taxation is the means through which this "leveling down process" is implemented. Taxes in the United States during the last decade have increased five hundred percent. If such increases continue, it will mean final confiscation of the property of the people."*

Joseph L. Wirthlin, Conference Report, April 1950, p.134

This process is what will have to be reversed if the Constitution is to be restored.

Conclusion

The constitutional restorations I've written about in this chapter are not the only possible ways of saving the Constitution. Certainly different methods may be employed to accomplish our task. I do know though that these are the vital portions of the Constitution that will need to be saved by those who step forward to defend our title of liberty. I know that because these are the areas cited by God's prophets as targets of our anxious engagement.

Chapter 16

"In memory of Our God, Our Religion, and Freedom, and Our Peace"

- **Our Title of Liberty**
- **Divided Into Thirds**
- **Are we part of the fence-sitting middle, or are we firmly on the Lord (and freedom's) side?**
- **Saving the Constitution is a spiritual battle**
- **Our Title of Liberty Moment**
- **"Where there is no vision…"**

Our Title of Liberty

I chose the title for this book not only because of its symbolism and applicability to our day, but also because of its dramatic 'moment-of-choosing' import. My hope is that everyone who reads it will take an honest look at his or her own convictions and then look to God for the courage to rally around His standard. The raising of the Title of Liberty was truly one of the most emotionally charged moments in the Book of Mormon. The free Nephite government, established by the people during the time of the great king and statesman Mosiah, hung in the balance. Amalickiah and his "kingmen" had apostatized from the true church and then tried to stir up the rest of the voters/citizens to destroy the government so that Amalickiah could be made king. When Captain Moroni heard of these dissensions he became angry at these usurpers, tore his coat off and wrote on it: "In memory of our God, our religion, and freedom, and our peace, our wives, and our children…" then fastened it to a pole and started waving it for all to see.

Imagine if you lived in one of the cities where Moroni paraded through with the Title of Liberty "crying with a loud voice, saying:

> *"Behold, whosoever will maintain this title upon the land, let them come forth in the strength of the Lord, and enter into a covenant that they will maintain their rights, and their religion, that the Lord God may bless them."* (Alma 46:20)

Imagine those that ignored him and continued working in the fields, thinking to themselves: "That Moroni—what an extremist. Amalickiah's not that bad. It doesn't really matter if Amalickiah or Nephihah's the chief judge." Now picture yourself on the correct side of that political question, hastening to answer the call to accompany Moroni, and then helping him accomplish the important work of restoring God's government. Now try and picture yourself answering that same call today.

You are needed to answer that call today. Our nation is being inundated by waves of evil influences, which in turn are weakening our nation's moral resolve and political institutions. Just as in Captain Moroni's day, our government's condition becomes more precarious as spiritual, moral, and family values become less and less important to many voters. That's why the Saints' rallying to save the Constitution is such an important prophecy. As a nation we are growing more divided and fractured as sides are chosen. However, *not all in the land have chosen their side yet!* Let's consider for a moment who these undecideds are.

Divided Into Thirds

At the national and state levels there is one constant in American two-party politics, and that is its back and forth nature in electing liberal leaning or conservative leaning governments. That's because the American voting public is roughly divided into thirds: conservatives, liberals, and swing-voters. Swing voters are people who do not always vote for the candidate of their party; (They are also referred to as independents or moderates.) In virtually every election, the republican and democrat parties receive enough votes from their base to get at least a third of the vote. Whether the country swings liberal or conservative depends on which party's candidate wins the hearts and minds of more than half of the swing voters. I imagine this was much the way it was in the preexistence. Right after the two plans were presented there was probably one third who knew Jesus' plan was the right one and another third firmly ensconced behind Satan's offering. Then the two sides battled for the remaining third. By virtue of the fact that it was the Savior, Adam, and choice spirits who conducted the war in heaven, all preexistent swing voters cast their ballot in favor of the Father's plan, hence the final tally of 66% to 33%.

That assumption makes sense when we remember that the prophet Abraham tells us that there were varying degrees of righteousness among the pre-existent spirits:

> "Now the Lord had shown unto me, Abraham, the intelligences that were organized before the world was; and among all these there were many of the noble and great ones;" (Abraham 3:22)

Bruce R. McConkie commented further on these varying degrees of spirits:

> "*The pre-existent life was thus a period—undoubtedly an infinitely long one—of probation, progression, and schooling. The spirit hosts were taught and given experiences in various administrative capacities. Some so exercised their agency and so conformed to law as to* **become** "*noble and great*"; *these were foreordained before their mortal births to perform great missions for the Lord in this life. (Abraham 3:22–28.)…Mortal progression and testing is a continuation of what began in pre-existence.*"
> Bruce R. McConkie, Mormon Doctrine, p.590 (bold, author's)

Our preexistent level of knowledge and righteousness in turn determined our circumstances in our second estate here on earth. I imagine that those varying levels of righteousness played their part in the war in heaven too, as some probably actively campaigned for our Father's Plan of Happiness, while others perhaps heard it and agreed, but did little beyond that.

Are we part of the fence-sitting middle, or are we firmly on the Lord (and freedom's) side?

From time to time it behooves us all to take personal inventory regarding where we stand in both our religion and our politics.

When it comes to our testimony of the church...

- Do we actively participate by accepting the calls that come to us?
- Do we actively magnify those callings?
- Are we "anxiously engaged...and bring[ing] to pass much righteousness?"

When it comes to our civic and political duties...

- Have we befriended the Constitution by studying and supporting its principles?
- Do we keep abreast of the issues and vote in all elections?
- Do we communicate our positions to our elected representatives, write letters to the editor, and spend a portion of our time trying to persuade others of our convictions?

Our answers to those questions will help us to identify in which third we make our own religious and political homes. My hopes in writing this book are that all of us who are not answering positively to these questions will take the necessary action to do so, and thus place ourselves among those with firm conviction. Once we decide to place ourselves in the top third, we must then do as President Benson counseled in his opening remarks of the October 1987 General Conference:

"How then can we best befriend the Constitution in this critical hour and secure the blessings of liberty and ensure the protection and guidance of our Father in Heaven? First and foremost, we must be righteous."

President Benson knew that the battle to save the Constitution, though outwardly political, would be fought on spiritual terms. Our own personal righteousness is our first, best weapon in this conflict.

Saving the Constitution is a spiritual battle

"If we ever forget that we're one nation under God, then we will be a nation gone under."
—Ronald Reagan (at prayer breakfast in Dallas, Texas, August 1984)

With the current assault on the Constitution, marriage, and the family, many are of the opinion that additional constitutional amendments are needed. While I would join in such efforts, I do not believe that passing more amendments will bring the Constitution back from the brink. Through the years we have witnessed the passing of various laws and measures, (e.g. the Defense of Marriage Act of 1995), and while they may slow the assault for the moment, they cannot replace the virtue that should reside in the hearts of the citizens. The just and holy principles of the Constitution rest upon the spiritual and moral character of the people, not the other way around.

Since this constitutional struggle is more spiritual than political, the choices are perhaps better defined not as between parties and programs, but between good and evil, life and death. Our generation's challenge is to combat the indifference and spiritual apathy that has infected much of our land. How are we to accomplish that goal? I believe that we will need to be actively engaged in being outspoken defenders of the Constitution at every available opportunity. That's exactly what Moroni did when he saw his country's freedom endangered. He took the principles that people had grown apathetic about and wrote them on his rent coat and waved it for all to see. As his fellow citizens read and remembered those important freedoms and how much they meant to them, they came rallying to the cause.

With that in mind, note the way President John Taylor expresses the method by which members of this church will save the Constitution:

> *"When the people shall have torn to shreds the Constitution of the United States, the elders of Israel will be found **holding it up to the nations of the earth** and proclaiming liberty and equal rights to all men, and extending the hand of fellowship to the oppressed of all nations. This is part of the program, and as long as we do what is right and fear God, he will help us and stand by us under all circumstances."*
> Journal of Discourses, 21:8, August 31, 1879. (bold, author's)

I believe that this "holding up" of the Constitution to the nations of the earth will not so much take place in the halls of Congress or the corridors of bureaucracies, but among the people. The Constitution will have to be defended in the hearts of the people first, then political victory will follow.

Our Title of Liberty Moment

Now that we know how the sides are divided up, and the terms on which the battle is to be fought, we need to uphold the Constitutions in our own lives. The time will come when current events will mirror the original Title of Liberty moment found in the 46th chapter of the book of Alma. When that crucial moment arrives let us take courage from those pioneers of American freedom...

> *12 And it came to pass that he [Captain Moroni] rent his coat; and he took a piece thereof, and wrote upon it—In memory of our God, our religion, and freedom, and our peace, our wives, and our children—and he fastened it upon the end of a pole.*
>
> *13 And he fastened on his head-plate, and his breastplate, and his shields, and girded on his armor about his loins; and he took the pole, which had on the end thereof his rent coat, (and he called it the title of liberty) and he bowed himself to the earth, and he prayed mightily unto his God for the blessings of liberty to rest upon his brethren, so long as there should a band of Christians remain to possess the land—*
>
> *14 For thus were all the true believers of Christ, who belonged to the church of God, called by those who did not belong to the church.*

Like Captain Moroni, we need to pray that our brethren feel the blessings of liberty rest upon them. We are that "band of Christians" left to possess the land promised to America's righteous inhabitants. Our invitation to others to join us in both Christianity and freedom will be a clarion call.

> *15 And those who did belong to the church were faithful; yea, all those who were true believers in Christ took upon them, gladly, the name of Christ, or Christians as they were called, because of their belief in Christ who should come.*
>
> *16 And therefore, at this time, Moroni prayed that the cause of the Christians, and the freedom of the land might be favored.*

Faithfulness in keeping God's commandments will determine the success of those who step forward to save the Constitution from destruction. Notice how Moroni prayed for the "cause of the Christians" in conjunction with the "freedom of the land." The message of the Gospel is inseparable from freedom and liberty. Missionary work will be a vital part of holding up the principles of the Constitution for all to see.

> *17 And it came to pass that when he had poured out his soul to God, he named all the land which was south of the land Desolation, yea, and in fine, all the land, both on the north and on the south—A chosen land, and the land of liberty.*
>
> *18 And he said: Surely God shall not suffer that we, who are despised because we*

take upon us the name of Christ, shall be trodden down and destroyed, until we bring it upon us by our own transgressions.

Pouring out our whole souls in prayer will be vital to our cause, because persecution against the cause of Christians will continue to grow. We are witnessing daily efforts to eliminate prayer and the Ten Commandments from public places. We see elected officials who profess belief in religion slandered as unfit or prejudiced in their public acts. This trend is not going to improve.

19 And when Moroni had said these words, he went forth among the people, waving the rent part of his garment in the air, that all might see the writing which he had written upon the rent part, and crying with a loud voice, saying:
20 Behold, whosoever will maintain this title upon the land, let them come forth in the strength of the Lord, and enter into a covenant that they will maintain their rights, and their religion, that the Lord God may bless them.

Since we live in a more technologically blessed dispensation than Captain Moroni, we have many means at our disposal whereby we can hold up the just and holy principles of the Constitution. We can support good and righteous messages in television and other media. We can campaign for wise and honest candidates not only by talking to friends and neighbors, but by email, phone, and fax correspondence. We can withhold our patronage from companies who sponsor constitutional deviation and we can give money to those who support the Constitution. Being anxiously engaged in all these endeavors will build up the numbers of people needed to restore the Constitution and its protections.

21 And it came to pass that when Moroni had proclaimed these words, behold, the people came running together with their armor girded about their loins, rending their garments in token, or as a covenant, that they would not forsake the Lord their God...
22...saying: We covenant with our God, that we shall be destroyed, even as our brethren in the land northward, if we shall fall into transgression; yea, he may cast us at the feet of our enemies, even as we have cast our garments at thy feet to be trodden under foot, if we shall fall into transgression.
28 And...when Moroni had said these words he went forth, and also sent forth in all the parts of the land where there were dissensions, and gathered together all the people who were desirous to maintain their liberty, to stand against Amalickiah and those who had dissented...

Through our efforts, all those who are prepared to defend and support the Constitution will gather together, ready to oppose those who would destroy it.

Finally, in verse twenty-nine, one of my personal favorites, we read about Moroni's victory, (note some of the similarities to the war in heaven):

> *29 And it came to pass that when Amalickiah saw that the people of Moroni were more numerous than the Amalickiahites—and he also saw that his people were doubtful concerning the justice of the cause in which they had undertaken—therefore, fearing that he should not gain the point, he took those of his people who would and departed into the land of Nephi.*

Just like Amalickiah's followers, those who wish to destroy the Constitution in our day, upon seeing the forces gathered to defend it, will doubt the justness of their cause and retreat. I believe that the Constitution will be saved in similar fashion. I don't think that necessarily means that we will be a majority, but I share Brigham Young's conviction when he said:

> *"Will the Constitution be destroyed? No: it will be held inviolate by this people; and, as Joseph Smith said, "The time will come when the destiny of the nation will hang upon a single thread. At that critical juncture, this people will step forth and save it from the threatened destruction."* **It will be so.***"*

Journal of Discourses, Vol.7, p.15, July 4, 1854 (bold, author's)

"Where there is no vision…"

The twenty-ninth chapter of Proverbs, 18th verse is one of my very favorite scriptures:

> *Where [there is] no vision, the people perish…*
> (Proverbs 29:18)

I believe that the term 'vision' is synonymous with "hope" in faith, hope, and charity. A clear vision of what we can be and who we can become if we are righteous is one of the strongest motivators we can have in our lives. That's why the writer of the proverbs equated lack of vision with perishing. People perish when they cannot see themselves winning life's struggle. Souls perish when they choose not to envision God's all encompassing love and longing for them to return his abode.

Politics is about vision too. The fates and destinies of nations have hinged upon the vision of great leaders that saw what could be and then inspired their brethren to see that same vision. This book is the vision of hope that I have received as I have studied the prophets and watched the signs of the times play out on the world stage. I know that if we follow the righteous examples of those who have gone before us, we will possess the same vision as the great prophets and founding fathers of the American nation. We will see this land as a refuge and respite for those who long to live free to follow God and his Christ. We will be prepared to sacrifice our own lives, fortunes, and sacred honor to be active in defending the principles that have sanctified it for this purpose. Most of all it is my hope that we all share the prophet Joseph's vision when he said…

> *"Hence we say, that the Constitution of the United States is a glorious standard; it is founded in the wisdom of God. It is a heavenly banner; it is to all those who are privileged with the sweets of liberty, like the cooling shades and refreshing waters of a great rock in a thirsty and weary land. It is like a great tree under whose branches men from every clime can be shielded from the burning rays of the sun."*

Letters of Joseph Smith, from Liberty Prison, March 25, 1839, History of the Church, Vol. III, p. 304.

If we do as the prophets have instructed, I know that when the time comes and the Constitution hangs by a thread that we will possess the faith, conviction and commitment to make us equal to our own Title of Liberty moment.

Appendix

▼

"And God said: These I will make my rulers; for he stood among those that were spirits, and he saw that they were good. (Abraham 3:23) And the Lord said: Whom shall I send? (Abraham 3:27) There stood one among them that was like unto God, and he said: (Abraham 3:24) "Father, thy will be done, and the glory be thine forever. (Moses 4:2) We will go down and we will make an earth whereon these may dwell; and we will prove them herewith, to see if they will do all things whatsoever the Lord their God shall command them." (Abraham 3:24–25)

And another answered and said: "Here am I, send me. (Abraham 3:27) I will be thy son, and I will redeem all mankind, that one soul shall not be lost, and surely I will do it; wherefore give me thine honor," (Moses 4:1) which is my power, (D&C 29:36) for he said in his heart: "I will ascend into heaven, (Isaiah 14:13) I will be like the most High; (Isaiah 14:14) I will exalt my throne above the stars of God." (Isaiah 14:13) And the Lord said: "I will send the first." And the second was angry, and kept not his first estate; (Abraham 3:27–28) and also a third part of the hosts of heaven turned he away from me because of their agency. (D&C 29:36)

And there was war in heaven; Michael and his angels fought against the dragon; and the dragon and his angels fought against Michael; and the dragon prevailed not against Michael (Revelations 12:7–8) for they overcame him by the blood of the Lamb, by the word of their testimony; for they loved not their own lives, but kept the testimony even unto death. (Revelations 12:11) Wherefore, because Satan rebelled against me, and sought to destroy the agency of man, which I, the

Lord God, had given him, by the power of mine Only Begotten, I caused that he should be cast down. (Moses 4:3) Thus Satan was cast out into the earth; and his angels were cast out with him. (Revelations 12:9) He became the devil, the father of all lies, to deceive and to blind men, and to lead them captive at his will, even as many as would not hearken unto my voice. (Moses 4:4) And he was called Perdition, for the heavens wept over him—he was Lucifer, a son of the morning!" (D&C 76:26)

Short List of 'Starter' Columnists

Conservative Columnists

George Will—a Pulitzer prize winner and one of the most often quoted by modern-day general authorities. His newspaper column has been syndicated by The Washington Post Writers Group since 1974.

Thomas Sowell—One of the best economists I've ever read. What's more, he can explain economics in a way the layman can understand. Dr. Sowell graduated magna cum laude from Harvard University (1958), then went on to receive his master's in economics from Columbia University (1959) and a doctorate in economics from the University of Chicago (1968).

Walter Williams—Another economist who can explain economics so that even the science and mathematically-challenged like myself can comprehend. He holds a bachelor's degree in economics from California State University (1965) and a master's degree (1967) and doctorate (1972) in economics from the University of California at Los Angeles. In 1980, he joined the faculty of George Mason University in Fairfax, Va., and is currently the John M. Olin Distinguished Professor of Economics.

Jonah Goldberg—A very funny personality who puts conservative politics in both an entertaining and thought-provoking context. *Caveat for the older reader:* Jonah is best understood by those in ages between 25–45. He uses a lot of Star Trek and Simpsons references in his humor

David Horowitz—Mr. Horowitz may be best known for his lifelong intellectual and political journey. He grew up in New York City as the son of two lifelong Communists, earned a Bachelor's degree from Columbia University in 1959 and a Master's degree from the University of California at Berkeley in 1961. Horowitz quickly became a leader of the New Left. During the '60s, Horowitz edited

Ramparts Magazine, an influential left-wing journal. He subsequently learned many of the left's follies the hard way and became a conservative.

John Podhoretz—Another conservative who was a left-leaning liberal in his early years. Mr. Podhoretz excels at explaining the whats, whys and wherefores of the opposition.

Brent Bozell—Mr. Bozell is an expert on media bias, among many other things. He is a lecturer, syndicated columnist, television commentator, debater, marketer, businessman, publisher and activist. In my opinion, he is one of the most effective spokesmen in the conservative movement today.

<u>Liberal Columnists</u>
Nat Hentoff—He received his B.A. with the highest honors from Northeastern University and did graduate work at Harvard. He has published many books on jazz, biographies and novels, including a number of books for children. Hentoff's views on journalistic responsibility and the rights of Americans to write, think and speak freely are expressed in his weekly column, and he has come to be acknowledged as a foremost authority in the area of First Amendment defense. He is also an expert on the Bill of Rights, the Supreme Court, student rights and education.

Mary McGrory—She captured the mood of Watergate in 1974, which earned her a Pulitzer Prize for commentary; discovered the best human interest story out of the Three Mile Island nuclear reactor accident; touched the hearts of millions with her prose following John Kennedy's assassination. Known for her long running analysis of Washington politics, her provocative and distinctive commentary appears three times each week in more than 125 papers around the country.

0-595-32533-5

Printed in the United States
22031LVS00004B/1-30